AS/A-LEVEL YEAR 1

STUDENT GUIDE

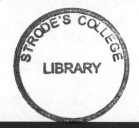

AQA

Politics

Government of the UK

Paul Fairclough and Nick Gallop

Series editor: Eric Magee

HODDER
EDUCATION
AN HACHETTE UK COMPANY

Hodder Education, an Hachette UK company, Blenheim Court, George Street, Banbury, Oxfordshire OX16 5BH

Orders

Bookpoint Ltd, 130 Park Drive, Milton Park, Abingdon, Oxfordshire OX14 4SB

tel: 01235 827720

fax: 01235 400401

e-mail: education@bookpoint.co.uk

Lines are open 9.00 a.m.–5.00 p.m., Monday to Saturday, with a 24-hour message answering service. You can also order through the Hodder Education website: www.hoddereducation.co.uk

© Paul Fairclough and Nick Gallop 2017

ISBN 978-1-4718-9296-7

First printed 2017

Impression number 5 4 3 2 1

Year 2021 2020 2019 2018 2017

This Guide has been written specifically to support students preparing for the AQA AS and A-level Politics examinations. The content has been neither approved nor endorsed by AQA and remains the sole responsibility of the author.

Cover photograph: sibgat/123 RF

Typeset by Integra Software Services Pvt. Ltd., Pondicherry, India

Printed in Italy

Hachette UK's policy is to use papers that are natural, renewable and recyclable products and made from wood grown in sustainable forests. The logging and manufacturing processes are expected to conform to the environmental regulations of the country of origin.

Contents

Getting the most from this book 4

About this book 5

Content Guidance

The nature and sources of the British Constitution 6

The structure and role of Parliament 22

The prime minister and cabinet 35

The judiciary 48

Devolution 59

Questions & Answers

6-mark questions (AS only)

The nature and sources of the British Constitution 72

The structure and role of Parliament 73

9-mark questions (A-level only)

The prime minister and cabinet 74

The judiciary 75

12-mark extract-based questions (AS only)

Devolution 77

The prime minister and cabinet 79

25-mark extract-based essay questions (A-level only)

The nature and sources of the British Constitution 81

The structure and role of Parliament 83

25-mark essay questions (AS and A-level)

The prime minister and cabinet 86

The judiciary 88

Knowledge check answers 90

Index 93

■Getting the most from this book

Exam tips

Advice on key points in the text to help you learn and recall content, avoid pitfalls, and polish your exam technique in order to boost your grade.

Knowledge check

Rapid-fire questions throughout the Content Guidance section to check your understanding.

Knowledge check answers

1 Turn to the back of the book for the Knowledge check answers.

Summaries

● Each core topic is rounded off by a bullet-list summary for quick-check reference of what you need to know.

Exam-style questions

Commentary on the questions

Tips on what you need to do to gain full marks, indicated by the icon ℮

Sample student answers

Practise the questions, then look at the student answers that follow.

Questions & Answers

■6-mark questions (AS only)

There are four of these questions on the AS paper which are assessed using AO1 only.

What do you need to do?
- Provide a clear and accurate definition of the concept, term or phrase identified in the question.
- Develop your explanation and demonstrate your deeper understanding by selecting and using appropriate examples in support of your answer.

The nature and sources of the British Constitution

Explain, with examples, the concept of an uncodified constitution.

℮ You should ensure that you have provided a clear and accurate definition of the term 'uncodified constitution' along with supporting examples that demonstrate what this means in practice. High-level responses will also demonstrate conceptual understanding of the difference between a constitution being 'uncodified' as opposed to 'unwritten' and contrast uncodified constitutions with the codified constitutions present in some states (e.g. the USA).

Student answer

A constitution is a set of fundamental rules (or 'fundamental law') that establishes the relationship between the state and the people, and also between those institutions that make up the state. An uncodified constitution differs from a codified constitution in that the key rules are brought together into a single, authoritative document. Codified constitutions normally result from some fundamental watershed in the history of a nation (e.g. new-found independence, war and occupation, or revolution) where people have sat down with a blank sheet of paper and tried to create a new model of government. This is true of countries such as the USA, Germany and France. The UK in contrast has an uncodified constitution that has evolved over time. It cannot be found in a single document but in a range of sources. It is wrong to see uncodified as meaning unwritten because some of these sources, like statute law, are written. Others, like conventions, are not. Uncodified constitutions tend to be easier to change whereas codified constitutions are often entrenched with complex amendment processes.

℮ Level 3 (6/6 marks awarded). This answer provides a clear definition. Although there is probably a little too much emphasis on codified constitutions, the material provides a sound foundation for the explanation of the term in question, which follows.

Commentary on sample student answers

Read the comments (preceded by the icon ℮) showing how many marks each answer would be awarded in the exam and exactly where marks are gained or lost.

■ About this book

The aim of this Student Guide is to prepare students for the Government of the UK section of AQA AS Paper 1 Government and Politics of the UK and AQA A-level Paper 1 Government and Politics of the UK.

For AS Politics students, the topics covered in this guide comprise half of the topics required for the examination on Government and Politics of the UK — they appear in the specification under the heading Government of the UK. For A-level Politics students, the topics covered in the guide form half of Paper 1 Government and Politics of the UK. A-level Politics Paper 1 represents a third of the papers required to complete the A-level examination. In both cases, all of the topics could be examined in the exam. It is therefore vital that you are familiar with and confident about all the material.

The **Content Guidance** section covers all the topics largely in the order in which they appear on the AQA AS and A-level specifications. You are strongly advised to have a copy of the specification to refer to as you go through the topics. For the section on the Government of the UK there are five main topics: The nature and sources of the British Constitution; The structure and role of Parliament; The prime minister and cabinet; The judiciary; and Devolution.

You should use the Content Guidance to ensure you are familiar with all the key concepts and terms, statistics, issues and arguments, and to give you a range of relevant examples that you can quote in your answers because you are aware of the relative significance of these principles and concepts. Throughout this section of the guide you will find definitions or explanations of important terms and concepts. There is also a series of knowledge checks which can act as a guide to some important examples you can use when answering questions and which will help to establish detailed knowledge. The answers to these knowledge checks can be found at the end of the guide. Exam tips are designed to help you avoid significant common errors made by students as well as guiding you towards good practice.

The **Questions & Answers** section is an opportunity to hone exam technique and to become familiar with the skills and structures that examiners are looking for in the AS and A-level exams. The answers illustrate both good and weak technique. It is not possible to provide sample questions and answers for each section of the exam on every topic, so you need to be aware that any parts of the specification could be tested in any sections of the examination.

This guide does not provide a full range of examples or go into full detail, so you should use it alongside other resources such as class notes and articles in *Politics Review* (published by Hodder Education). You should also use websites such as the BBC, TotalPolitics.com, The Times Red Box and www.politics.co.uk to keep up to date with current news.

Content Guidance

■ The nature and sources of the British Constitution

What is a constitution?

A constitution is a body of laws, rules and practices that sets out the way in which a state or society is organised:

- It defines the relationship between the state and its citizens.
- It establishes the institutions that constitute the state and regulates relations between them.

In a **democracy**, the constitution provides for **limited government**, guaranteeing citizens certain key rights and defending against any abuse of power by the state, its institutions or its officials.

Codified and uncodified constitutions

We tend to draw a distinction between those which are 'codified' and those that remain 'uncodified'.

A codified constitution is a single, authoritative document that sets out the laws, rules and principles by which a state is governed, and protects the rights of citizens, e.g. the UK Constitution.

An uncodified constitution is a constitution where the laws, rules and principles specifying how a state is to be governed are not gathered in a single document. Instead they are found in a variety of sources, some written and some unwritten, e.g. the US Constitution.

Features of codified constitutions

Codified constitutions are generally produced at a critical juncture in a nation's history, most commonly in the wake of:

- new-found independence, e.g. the US Constitution of 1789
- a period of authoritarian rule, e.g. the Spanish Constitution of 1978
- war and/or occupation, e.g. West Germany's Basic Law of 1949.

In such situations, a new constitution is afforded the status of **fundamental law**, or 'higher law'. This means that it is placed above ordinary law made by the legislature (or 'parliament') and is said to be **entrenched**. In countries with codified constitutions, a constitutional court (or 'supreme court') has the job of holding other key players, whether individuals or institutions, accountable to this supreme law.

State A collective term referring to all the institutions of government that operate within a country and exercise power over its citizens.

Democracy Derived from the Greek *dēmokratia*, which is a combination of *dēmos* (meaning 'the people') and *kratos* (meaning 'power'). Literally, therefore, democracy is 'rule by the people' or 'people power'.

Limited government System of government under which the powers of the state are subject to legal constraints, and checks and balances within the political system.

Fundamental law Constitutional law that is deliberately set above regular statute in terms of status and given a degree of protection against regular laws passed by the legislature.

Entrenched Made difficult to change (literally 'dug in'); often requiring supermajorities — or approval by popular referendum.

The UK Constitution

The UK has an uncodified constitution. Although it is frequently described as 'unwritten', this is misleading because while the nation's constitutional practices and principles are not gathered in a single authoritative document, many are 'written' in 'common law' (the decisions of the higher courts) and others can be found in 'statute law' (Acts of Parliament) or other key historical documents (see Table 1).

Table 1 Five key historical documents

Act or measure	Significance
Magna Carta (1215)	Guaranteed the right to a swift and fair trial Placed limitations on taxation
Bill of Rights (1689)	Limited the power of the monarch and enhanced the status of Parliament Prohibited cruel and unusual punishment
Act of Settlement (1701)	Barred Roman Catholics or those married to Roman Catholics from taking the throne Resulted in the House of Hanover assuming the English throne Paved the way for the Acts of Union (1707), which united the kingdoms of England and Scotland to form Great Britain, governed from Westminster
Parliament Acts (1911/1949)	Two Acts of Parliament that effectively removed the power of the House of Lords to block money bills Reduced the upper chamber's ability to delay non-money bills to one year
European Communities Act (1972)	The Act of Parliament that formally took the UK into the European Economic Community (EEC) Made European law superior to domestic law

The sources of the British Constitution

Uncodified constitutions, as we have seen, tend to draw on a range of sources — some written and some unwritten. In the case of the UK Constitution it is possible to identify five such sources:

1 Statute law.

2 Common law.

3 Conventions.

4 Authoritative opinions (or 'works of authority').

5 European Union law and treaties.

Statute law

Statute law consists of laws created by Parliament in the form of Acts of Parliament. These Acts are implemented (or 'executed') by the executive and enforced by the courts. Although not all Acts of Parliament are of constitutional significance, statute law is the supreme source of constitutional law in the UK — because Parliament is sovereign.

Examples of recent pieces of statute law that have been of historical importance in constitutional terms include:

■ the Scotland Act (1998), which created a Scottish Parliament

■ the Human Rights Act (1998), which incorporated the rights set out in the European Convention on Human Rights (ECHR) into UK law

Knowledge check 1

Using the information provided as well as your own research, write two paragraphs:

● One paragraph should argue the case in favour of codified constitutions.

● The other paragraph should argue the case in favour of uncodified constitutions.

Knowledge check 2

Explain, using examples, why it is wrong to describe the UK Constitution as 'unwritten'.

- the Constitutional Reform Act (CRA) (2005), which established the UK Supreme Court and the Judicial Appointments Commission
- the Fixed-term Parliaments Act (2011), which established fixed, five-yearly elections to the Westminster Parliament.

Common law

Common law is created when judges in the UK's higher courts use their power of judicial review to clarify or establish a legal position where statute law is unclear. This 'case law' or 'judge-made law' forms a body of legal precedent that serves to guide both the lower courts and future lawmakers. The phrase 'common law' is also taken to include customs and precedents that have come to be seen as legally binding. One good example of this is the royal prerogative, the powers exercised in the name of the Crown.

Conventions

Conventions are accepted norms of behaviour. Although they are not legally enforceable, their usage over an extended period of time gives conventions a degree of authority. For example, the monarch, by convention, must give their assent to Acts of Parliament. No monarch has refused to give their assent since 1707, when Queen Anne refused to approve the Scottish Militias Bill. Thus, if the monarch were to refuse a bill today, there would be a constitutional crisis.

While conventions may fall into disuse over time, new conventions can also be established. For example, during his short tenure as prime minister, Gordon Brown announced that the UK would not declare war without a parliamentary vote.

Authoritative opinions (or 'works of authority')

There is a handful of authoritative works that has come to be accepted as the 'go-to' references for knowing precisely 'who' can do 'what' under the UK Constitution. While these texts hold no formal legal status, they do have 'persuasive authority'. Such works of authority include:

- Erskine May's *Treatise on the Law, Privileges, Proceedings and Usage of Parliament* (1844)
- Walter Bagehot's *The English Constitution* (1867)
- A.V. Dicey's *Introduction to the Study of the Law of the Constitution* (1885).

European Union law

The UK became a member of the European Economic Community (EEC) in 1973, under the terms of the European Communities Act (1972). The Maastricht Treaty (1991) transformed this Economic Community into the European Union (EU) from 1993.

As a full member of the EU, the UK is subject both to its laws and to the judgments of the European Court of Justice, the EU's 'supreme court'. In short, EU law takes precedence over UK law. The decision to trigger Article 50 in the wake of the 2016 referendum, and thereby start the process of negotiating the UK's withdrawal from the EU, will ultimately remove this fifth source of the UK Constitution.

Common law Law derived from general customs or traditions and the decision of judges.

Judicial review In the UK context, the power of senior judges to review the actions of government and public authorities, declaring them unlawful if they have exceeded their authority.

Royal prerogative Those constitutional powers that are still technically held by the monarch traditionally but are exercised in practice by the prime minister or other government ministers.

Conventions Established norms of political behaviour, rooted in past experience rather than the law.

The principles that underpin the UK Constitution

Four key principles are said to underpin the UK Constitution:

1 Parliamentary sovereignty.
2 The rule of law.
3 A unitary state.
4 Parliamentary government under a constitutional monarchy.

Parliamentary sovereignty

Parliamentary sovereignty is the cornerstone of the UK Constitution.

The doctrine of parliamentary sovereignty is constructed around three interconnected propositions:

- that Parliament can legislate on any subject of its choosing
- that parliamentary statute cannot be overturned by any higher authority
- that no Parliament can bind its successors.

The rule of law

The rule of law is an essential feature of a liberal democracy. According to the nineteenth-century constitutional lawyer A.V. Dicey (1885), the rule of law has three main strands:

- First, that no man can be punished without trial.
- Second, that no one is above the law, and all are subject to the same justice.
- Third, that the general principles of the Constitution, such as personal freedoms, result from judge-made common law rather than from parliamentary statute or executive order.

A unitary state

We routinely draw a distinction between those constitutions that concentrate ultimate political power at the centre (unitary constitutions) and those that divide it between central and regional tiers of government (federal constitutions).

A unitary state is a state in which sovereignty is located at the centre. Central government has supremacy over other tiers of government, which it can reform or abolish.

A federal state is a state in which sovereignty is divided between two or more tiers of government. Most commonly, power is shared between national government (the federal government) and regional government (the states). Regional government is afforded protection by the Constitution: it cannot be abolished or reformed significantly against its will.

The traditional British constitution is a unitary constitution. Although the United Kingdom consists of four component nations — England, Scotland, Wales and Northern Ireland — it has been a highly centralised state in which legal sovereignty is retained by the Westminster Parliament.

It is important to note the distinction between true federalism and the situation that exists in the UK following devolution. Under a truly federal system, sovereignty is divided between different tiers of government; powers are not simply delegated or devolved by central government.

Parliamentary sovereignty The doctrine that Parliament has absolute legal authority within the state. It enjoys legislative supremacy: Parliament may make law on any matter it chooses, its decisions may not be overturned by any higher authority and it may not bind its successors.

Knowledge check 3

Explain briefly why the UK was traditionally said to be a unitary state.

Parliamentary government under a constitutional monarchy

Under the UK Constitution, government takes place through Parliament under a **constitutional monarchy**.

Government ministers are politically accountable to Parliament and legally accountable to the Crown, and must also face the verdict of the electorate every five years. Between general elections, a government relies upon its majority in the House of Commons (the 'confidence of the Commons') both to survive and to enact its legislative programme.

Constitutional monarchy
Political system in which the monarch is the formal head of state but the monarch's legal powers are exercised by government ministers.

Issues and debates around recent constitutional changes

What changes have been made to the Constitution since 1997?

The UK's traditional constitution is known as 'the **Westminster model**'. While supporters of this model recognise that some improvements may be required, they believe that any reform should be limited and pragmatic. Any changes should be made within the broad framework of the existing Constitution, rather than seeking to totally overhaul it. In contrast, critics of the traditional Constitution argue that the existing model has a number of serious weaknesses that could be remedied only by a significant reform programme of the type embarked upon by the Labour Party between 1997 and 2010.

Westminster model
Form of government exemplified by the British political system, in which Parliament is sovereign, the executive and legislature are fused and political power is centralised.

Constitutional reform under New Labour (1997–2010)

The Labour Party went into the 1997 general election promising a programme of radical constitutional reform that was driven by four interlocking themes:

■ Modernisation: reform for institutions such as Parliament, the executive and the civil service.
■ Democratisation: encouraging greater participation in the political process.
■ Decentralisation: the devolution of decision-making powers to new institutions in Scotland and Wales, with the role of local government also being enhanced.
■ Rights: enhanced rights for citizens.

The changes that the party put in place following its victory in that election went some way towards addressing these four themes (see Table 2).

Table 2 Constitutional reform 1997–2010

Area	Reform
Rights	The Human Rights Act (1998) The Freedom of Information Act (2000)
Devolution	A Scottish Parliament with primary legislative and tax-raising powers A Northern Ireland Assembly with primary legislative powers A Welsh Assembly with secondary legislative powers

Area	Reform
Decentralisation	A directly elected mayor of London and London Assembly, and elected mayors in some English authorities
Electoral reform	New electoral systems for devolved assemblies, European Parliament and mayoral elections
Parliament	All but 92 hereditary peers removed from the House of Lords Limited reforms to the workings of the House of Commons
Judiciary	The Constitutional Reform Act (2005), which resulted in: ● a new UK Supreme Court ● a new judicial appointments system ● changes to the role of Lord Chancellor ● the creation of a new Justice Department
Participation	Wider use of referendums Political Parties, Elections and Referendums Act (2000) regulated the conduct of parties and elections

Of the changes made by New Labour, those in respect of devolution, the House of Lords and human rights were, perhaps, the most significant.

Devolution

In 1999, power was devolved to new institutions in Scotland, Wales and Northern Ireland, following 'yes' votes in referendums in each nation. The new system was one of asymmetric devolution rather than following a standardised blueprint; the devolved bodies were granted different powers and distinctive features. Devolution was to be a process rather than an event, with further powers devolved since 1999.

Scottish Parliament

The Scottish Parliament has primary legislative and tax-varying powers. The Parliament, together with the Scottish Executive, has sole responsibility for policy on issues such as education, health and local government. Granting such wide-ranging powers to the Scottish government while still allowing Scottish MPs at Westminster to vote on laws that no longer directly affected their constituents brought the so-called **West Lothian question** into sharp focus.

Welsh Assembly

The National Assembly for Wales, commonly referred to as the Welsh Assembly, was initially weaker than the Scottish Parliament. It had secondary legislative and executive powers, but no primary legislative authority. This meant that it could 'fill in the details' of, and implement, legislation passed by the Westminster Parliament only in policy areas such as education and health.

Northern Ireland Assembly

The Northern Ireland Assembly was granted legislative powers over a similar range of policy areas as the Scottish Parliament but was not given tax-raising powers. Special procedures were established in the Assembly to ensure cross-community support. These included the establishment of a power-sharing executive.

West Lothian question
Originally posed by Labour MP Tam Dalyell in a Commons debate back in 1977, the West Lothian question asks: Why should Scottish MPs be able to vote on English matters at Westminster when English MPs cannot vote on matters devolved to the Scottish Parliament?

Knowledge check 4

Explain why, even after devolution, it would still not be accurate to describe the UK as operating under a federal system.

Quasi-federalism

While these changes clearly did not turn the UK into a truly federal system, for the reasons identified earlier in this section, some used the term 'quasi-federalism' when seeking to attach a label to the state of affairs that resulted from New Labour's devolution programme.

Quasi-federalism is when the central government of a unitary state devolves some of its powers to subnational governments. It exhibits some of the features of a unitary state and some of a federal state. In legal theory there is one supreme legal authority located at the centre, as in a unitary state. But in practice the centre no longer makes domestic policy for some parts of the state and it would be difficult politically for the centre to abolish the subnational tier of government. Different policy frameworks operate within the state. Senior judges rule on questions concerning the division of competences.

Changing composition of the House of Lords

The House of Lords Act (1999) abolished the right of all but 92 hereditary peers (i.e. those who inherited their titles) to sit and vote in the upper house. This was intended as the first stage of the reform process. The Lords now comprised mainly life peers, and no political party had an overall majority. But the Labour governments made little progress with 'stage two' of the reforms, when the final composition and powers of the reformed House of Lords would be settled. Although various papers and a number of bills were brought forward for debate in the years that followed, there was a fundamental division between the Commons and the Lords on how reform should progress, with the Commons generally favouring a partially or entirely elected second chamber and the Lords favouring an appointed model.

The Human Rights Act

The Human Rights Act (HRA, 1998) enshrined most of the provisions of the European Convention on Human Rights in UK law.

> **ECHR guarantees**
>
> - The right to life.
> - The right to liberty and personal security.
> - The right to a fair trial.
> - Respect for private and family life.
> - Freedom of thought and expression.
> - Freedom of peaceful assembly and association.
> - The right to marry and start a family.
> - Freedom from torture and degrading treatment.
> - Freedom from discrimination.

The HRA requires the British government to ensure that legislation is compatible with the Convention. Before the HRA, cases were heard by the European Court of Human Rights (ECtHR) in Strasbourg. Although UK courts can now hear cases under the Convention, they cannot automatically overturn legislation that they deem to be incompatible with its provisions: it is up to Parliament to decide whether or not

Exam tip

As well as using the term 'quasi-federalism' as a way of explaining our constitutional arrangements post-devolution, writers such as Vernon Bogdanor have described the UK as a 'nation of nations'.

Knowledge check 5

Using the information in this book and your own research, explain why it has proven impossible to complete the second stage of Lords reform.

to amend or repeal the offending statute. We will be returning to the theme of rights and civil liberties towards the end of this section of the guide.

Constitutional reform after New Labour

The coalition and constitutional reform (2010–15)

Coalition governments inevitably involve a degree of compromise and the Conservative–Lib Dem administration in power between 2010 and 2015 was no exception to that rule. Although some significant changes were made to the UK's constitutional arrangements, most of the other significant changes proposed in the 2010 Coalition Agreement stalled (e.g. Lords reform) or were approved only in a watered-down form (e.g. the Recall of MPs Act). Of the changes that were made under the coalition, only five can be seen as worthy of more detailed consideration.

Fixed-term Parliaments Act (2011)

This Act established a pattern of fixed general elections every five years, starting in 2015. It thereby removed the ability of the prime minister to use the monarch's prerogative powers in order to call an election at a politically advantageous time.

However, it must be noted that the prime minister still has the power to dissolve Parliament and call a general election. On 18 April 2017 Theresa May announced that she intended to call a general election for 8 June 2017. She required a two-thirds Commons majority to do so and, with the support of the Labour Party, achieved this by 522 votes to 13. The Act requires elections to take place on the first Thursday in May no later than 5 years after the previous one. If no general election is called earlier, the next one will take place on 5 May 2022.

Scotland Act (2012)

This Act gave the Scottish government the power to vary income tax up or down by 10% as well as devolving further powers to the Scottish government — for example, the regulation of controlled drugs. The Act also allowed the Scottish government to borrow up to £2.2 billion each year.

Protection of Freedoms Act (2012)

This Act offered citizens greater protection from the state by putting in place proper scrutiny of the security services and oversight of surveillance and data collection. It was seen as necessary in light of the avalanche of anti-terrorist control measures in the wake of 9/11.

House of Lords Reform Act (2014)

By giving existing peers the right to retire or resign their seats in the chamber, this Act aimed to slow the increase in the number of those eligible to sit and vote in the House of Lords. It also allowed peers to be removed as a result of serious criminal offences or non-attendance: 58 peers had resigned under the terms of the Act by April 2017; a further four were removed as a result of non-attendance.

Wales Act (2014)

The Wales Act was the UK government's response to the Silk Commission's recommendations on further devolution to Wales. Although it was fairly modest in scope, the Act did transfer control of some smaller taxes to devolved institutions in

Knowledge check 6

Explain the significance of the decision to remove the prime minister's power to call a general election at a time of their choosing under the Fixed-term Parliaments Act.

Wales. It also put in place a mechanism by which other lower-level taxes could be devolved, with the approval of the Westminster Parliament, and provided the legal framework required for a Welsh referendum on the partial devolution of income tax. Symbolically, the Act changed the name of the Welsh Executive from the Welsh Assembly Government to the Welsh Government.

The Conservatives and constitutional reform (2015–)

Although the Conservative Party's 2015 general election manifesto made few promises in the area of constitutional reform, the party had delivered on most of its pledges within two years of taking office.

Scotland Act (2016) and Wales Act (2017)

The Scotland Act (2016) gave the Scottish government greater fiscal (i.e. financial) autonomy (see below) and the Wales Act (2017) reinforced the primary legislative authority that devolved institutions in Wales had been granted in the wake of the 2011 Welsh referendum. This Act also paved the way for the National Assembly of Wales to set Welsh rates of income tax from April 2019 — without the need for the kind of referendum envisaged under the Wales Act (2014).

The Scotland Act (2016)

This Act put into place many of the recommendations of the Smith Commission, the body established in the immediate aftermath of the 2014 Scottish independence referendum.

The Act made a number of significant changes:

- Devolved institutions were granted new powers over taxation, being allowed to set the rates and thresholds for income tax as well as gaining control of 50% of VAT levies.
- The result of these changes meant that, for the first time, the Scottish government was responsible for raising more than 50% of the money that it spends.
- The Scottish Parliament was given legislative power over a range of new areas, including road signs, speed limits and some welfare benefits.
- The Scottish government was given control over its electoral system, although a two-thirds supermajority in the Scottish Parliament was required for any change.
- Crucially, the Act also recognised the permanence of devolved institutions in Scotland and determined that a referendum would be required before either the Scottish Parliament or the Scottish government could be abolished.

The Barnett formula and 'English votes for English laws'

The Barnett formula is the funding mechanism devised in 1978 by the then Chief Secretary to the Treasury, Labour MP Joel Barnett. This formula translates changes in public spending in England into equivalent changes in the block grants for Scotland, Wales and Northern Ireland, calculated on the basis of population. Under the formula, these nations had higher public spending per person than England.

Although the controversial Barnett formula was left in place in the wake of the Scotland and Wales Acts and earlier reforms, English MPs have now been given special privileges when dealing with those matters affecting England alone — a form of 'English votes for English laws'.

The 2013 report of the 'Commission on the consequences of devolution for the House of Commons' (also known as the McKay Commission) recommended that only English MPs should be allowed to vote on measures which were identified as affecting only England. Changes to House of Commons standing orders made in the wake of the 2015 general election mean that this form of 'English votes for English laws' is now in place. The new system was used for the first time in January 2016, when only those MPs representing English constituencies were permitted to vote on some elements of a Housing and Planning Bill.

Brexit

It is worth remembering that as well as delivering on its manifesto promises as regards subnational government, the Conservative government, by staging an 'in/out' referendum on UK membership of the EU, has delivered on an earlier promise that, as we have already noted, could have significant implications for the UK's constitutional arrangements.

Rights in the UK

What do we mean by rights?

A **right** is a legal or moral entitlement to behave in a particular way. In the context of politics, the term 'rights' is often used interchangeably with the phrase **civil liberties**. Civil liberties are those fundamental freedoms that are enjoyed by citizens under the style of limited government practised in most liberal democracies.

As Paul Floyd has noted, such liberties may concern the freedom 'to do' or 'to have' something, such as the right to assemble, to privacy, to ownership of property or to a fair trial, or, alternatively, may be about freedom 'from' things, such as oppression, arbitrary arrest, slavery or imprisonment without trial. In theory, at least, government should limit (abrogate) such liberties only in time of war or other national emergency.

The main rights and liberties available to UK citizens are no different from those granted to citizens living in other liberal democratic states: the right to life, freedom of expression, freedom of religion and conscience, freedom of movement, freedom of association, the right of protest, freedom from arbitrary arrest, freedom from torture, right to a fair trial, political rights — for example, the right to vote (the franchise) — and property rights.

Debates about the extent of rights in the UK

Where are the rights of UK citizens set out?

The uncodified nature of the UK's constitutional arrangements has traditionally made it harder to determine precisely 'where' rights and liberties are set out. Historically, the UK has had neither a codified constitution nor, prior to 1998, anything akin to

Right Legal or moral entitlement to have something or behave in a particular way.

Civil liberties The fundamental freedoms enjoyed by citizens in a liberal democracy, limited only by those laws that have been established for the common good.

the US Bill of Rights. Instead, the Constitution has evolved over time, with citizens remaining technically free to do anything that is not prohibited in statute, a system characterised by **negative rights** as opposed to **positive rights**.

According to A.V. Dicey, statute law has only a relatively minor role to play in defending the civil liberties of UK citizens. Dicey maintained that such freedoms were instead protected:

- through the actions of a sovereign, independent and robust parliament, that would act quickly to remedy injustices
- through the laying down of judge-made 'case law' (common law)
- by the fact that public opinion would not stand for the government encroaching upon long-standing freedoms.

This meant that UK citizens' rights were traditionally protected by an overlapping web of provisions, some rooted in convention, some afforded statutory footing and others resulting from legal precedents established in the courts. For example, the right to life — long established in common law — was also recognised in parliamentary statutes such as the Offences Against the Persons Act (1861), the Murder (Abolition of Death Penalty) Act (1965) and the Crime and Disorder Act (1998), as well as in a number of international treaties and conventions, for example Protocol 13 (2002) of the European Convention on Human Rights and the United Nations Convention on the Rights of the Child (1989).

Contemporary legislation and current issues regarding rights

The lack of any clear and authoritative summary of the rights available to UK citizens led New Labour to bring two key pieces of legislation into law in the wake of the party's victory in the 1997 general election: the Human Rights Act (1998) and the Freedom of Information Act (2000).

The Human Rights Act (HRA, 1998)

The HRA (1998) came into force in October 2000. It incorporated most of the Articles of the ECHR into UK law, thereby allowing citizens to pursue cases under the ECHR through UK courts as opposed to having to go directly to the ECtHR in Strasbourg.

The European Convention on Human Rights (ECHR, 1950)

The ECHR was established by the Council of Europe, an intergovernmental body that is separate from the European Union and not to be confused with the EU's Council of Ministers or European Council. Alleged violations of the ECHR are investigated by the European Commission on Human Rights and tried in the European Court of Human Rights, based in Strasbourg.

As the HRA is based on the Council of Europe's ECHR rather than on EU law, it is not superior to parliamentary statute, as EU laws have been under the Treaty of Rome. That said, the HRA (like the ECHR) has a 'persuasive authority' that has enhanced the protection of individual rights in the UK.

Negative rights Those liberties that are not explicitly set out but exist in the absence of any law forbidding individuals from exercising them.

Positive rights Those rights explicitly assigned to citizens, often being entrenched as part of a codified constitutional settlement, as is the case in the USA.

Exam tip

Avoid confusing the European Court of Human Rights (ECtHR) with the European Court of Justice (ECJ).

The ECtHR was established by the Council of Europe to hear cases brought under the ECHR. It is based in Strasbourg but is not an EU institution.

The ECJ is the 'supreme court' of the European Union. It hears cases arising under EU law and is based in Luxembourg.

The HRA in outline

- The HRA (1998) came into force in October 2000.
- It incorporated most of the Articles of the 1950 ECHR into UK law.
- It included the right to life (Article 2), the right to liberty and security (Article 5), the right to a fair trial (Article 6), the right to family and private life (Article 8), the freedom of expression (Article 10) and protection against discrimination (Article 14).
- The HRA is based on the Council of Europe's ECHR rather than on EU law, so it is not superior to parliamentary statute, as EU laws are under the Treaty of Rome.

The HRA in action

As a regular piece of statute the HRA can be amended, 'suspended' (derogated) — in its entirety or in part — or simply repealed, like any other Act. Derogation is the process by which a country is exempted, perhaps temporarily, from observing a law or regulation it has previously agreed to abide by. Under Article 15 of the European Convention on Human Rights, national governments are permitted to derogate some of the Convention's articles in times of national crisis.

However, while the courts cannot strike down an Act of Parliament under the HRA, they can make a declaration of incompatibility and invite Parliament to reconsider the offending statute. Furthermore, where statute law is silent or unclear, the courts can make even greater use of the HRA by using its provisions to establish legal precedents in common law.

It is important to remember that the HRA also has a hidden influence through the process by which draft legislation is now examined by Parliament's Joint Committee on Human Rights in order to ensure that it will be compatible with the rights incorporated.

The courts, the HRA and the detention of terrorist suspects

Part 4 of the UK's Anti-terrorism, Crime and Security Act (2001) allowed the indefinite detention of foreign terrorist suspects without trial. It could be passed into law only because the government chose to derogate Article 5 of the European Convention on Human Rights on the grounds that there was a 'public emergency threatening the life of the nation'.

In the landmark case *A and Others v. Secretary of State for the Home Department* (2004), senior judges ruled that the indefinite detention of suspects under the Anti-terrorism, Crime and Security Act (2001) was incompatible with Articles 5 and 14 of the HRA. In June and August 2006 the High Court found that the use of control orders allowed under the Prevention of Terrorism Act (2005) also violated Article 5 because such restrictive measures amounted to imprisonment without trial.

Indefinite detention The right to hold foreign terrorist suspects indefinitely without trial as authorised by the Anti-terrorism, Crime and Security Act (2001). Suspects were famously held at Belmarsh Prison in London. Indefinite detention was ruled incompatible with the Human Rights Act (1998) in the case *A and Others v. Secretary of State for the Home Department* (2004).

Control order Form of close house arrest allowed under the Prevention of Terrorism Act (2005). Introduced after the indefinite detention of foreign terrorist suspects, sanctioned under the Anti-terrorism, Crime and Security Act (2001), was declared incompatible with the ECHR incorporated into UK law under the Human Rights Act (1998).

Freedom of Information Act (FOI, 2000)

The FOI was a direct response to the widespread perception that there needed to be greater transparency in government.

The Freedom of Information Act (FOI) in outline

- The FOI (2000) came into force in January 2005.
- It gave citizens a right to access information held by public authorities.
- It required public bodies seeking to deny requests for information to show that the public interest warrants an exemption under the Act.
- It established a new Information Commissioner and Information Tribunal.
- It required public authorities to adopt a scheme for the publication of information.

The Act received the Royal Assent on 30 November 2000 but did not come into force until 1 January 2005. This delay in implementation was supposed to provide public authorities an opportunity to prepare for the anticipated avalanche of requests for information.

The FOI in action

Public authorities ranging from government departments to local police and fire authorities had spent five years preparing for 'information D-day' on 1 January 2005. Indeed, in many cases additional staff had been taken on specifically to deal with requests from the public. However, the FOI (2000) did not lead to the anticipated avalanche of requests for information.

Most early requests under the Act came not from individual citizens but from media organisations that saw the Act as an additional tool when engaged in investigative journalism. By 2010, however, the FOI had been used far more widely and was increasingly seen as an effective means by which the government and elected officials could be held to account.

In no area was the use of the FOI more apparent than in the case of the furore over MPs' expenses in 2009. Though this scandal entered the broader public consciousness as a result of the *Daily Telegraph*'s decision to publish in full leaked details of MPs' expenses, we should remember that the chain of events that led to this outcome began with an FOI request by the Anglo-American journalist Heather Brooke in 2008.

Areas where individual and collective rights are in agreement and in conflict

The status of rights in the UK

As we have seen, the UK courts cannot declare an Act of Parliament unconstitutional as a result of the supremacy of statute law. The power of senior judges is therefore limited to declaring that a government official has acted beyond the authority given to them under statute (ultra vires), suspending UK statutes where they appear to violate EU law (since the **Factortame** case) or issuing a declaration of incompatibility where the measures in question appear to violate the HRA (1998). That said, it is important not to underestimate the significance of **political culture** when assessing the extent to

Knowledge check 7

Using examples, explain why the passing of laws such as the HRA (1998) and the FOI (2000) has not undermined the doctrine of parliamentary sovereignty.

Factortame A case in which the European Court of Justice established the precedent that UK courts can suspend UK statute law where it appears to violate EU law, at least until the ECJ is able to make a final determination as to the legality of the statute in question.

Political culture The opinions, attitudes and values that shape political behaviour. A nation's political culture consists of the citizens' collectively held attitudes towards the political system and their place in it.

which a government is able to encroach upon individual liberties unchallenged, as we noted earlier when considering A.V. Dicey's views.

It is clearly unrealistic to think that UK political culture would be transformed overnight as a result of the passage of measures such as the HRA (1998) and the FOI (2000). It takes time for the provisions of such Acts to enter the public consciousness and longer still before ordinary citizens feel confident in exercising such rights when seeking legal redress. However, while early cases saw the HRA being used largely by celebrities as a means of protecting their privacy, as opposed to ordinary citizens protecting their civil liberties, recent years have seen more widespread and ground-breaking use both of this Act and of the FOI (2000).

Threats to civil liberties post 9/11

The lack of entrenchment afforded to citizens' rights in the UK was highlighted by the erosion of individual liberties that came in the wake of the terrorist attacks in the USA on 9/11 (2001) and in London on 7/7 (2005). Caught between the need to protect the lives of UK citizens and a desire to protect individual rights and liberties, the government often appeared to prioritise the former over the latter when framing legislation (see Table 3).

Table 3 Civil liberties under threat post 9/11

Act	Year	Key provisions
Anti-terrorism, Crime and Security Act	2001	Allowed the indefinite detention of foreign terrorist suspects
Proceeds of Crime Act	2002	Allowed the confiscation of the assets of suspected terrorists without prosecution
Regulation of Investigatory Powers Act	2002	Empowered the police and local authorities to undertake covert surveillance
Criminal Justice Act	2003	Limited the right to trial by jury in some cases
Prevention of Terrorism Act	2005	Introduced control orders
Serious Organised Crime and Police Act	2005	Restricted protests in the vicinity of Parliament
Terrorism Act	2006	Made it an offence to 'glorify' acts of terrorism
Counter-Terrorism Act	2008	Allowed the police to restrict photography in public places as well as extending the rights of police to take DNA evidence and monitor those suspected of involvement in terrorism activity
Coroners and Justice Act	2009	Allowed inquests into deaths relating to terrorist activities to be held in secret

The philosopher John Locke (1632–1704) recognised that in an emergency 'responsible leaders could resort to exceptional power' — and it is certainly true that citizens will often defer to government in times of national emergency, accepting restrictions on civil liberties that they would surely never countenance in the normal course of events.

Once passed into law, however, it is up to the authorities to determine precisely how such powers are applied and when (if ever) they are rescinded. The open-ended nature of many of the measures that found their way onto the statute books in the early part of the twenty-first century presented a clear and present danger to civil liberties in the

Exam tip

The draconian restrictions on protests in the vicinity of Parliament that were introduced as part of the Serious Organised Crime and Police Act (2005) were aimed at ending peace campaigner Brian Haw's long-running anti-war protest in Parliament Square. The restrictions were repealed as part of the Police Reform and Social Responsibility Act (2011).

UK. Moreover, it was a threat that was not removed by the repeal of some acts (see below) or the coalition's Protection of Freedoms Act (2012).

Does the UK need a formal Bill of Rights?

Controversy over the Human Rights Act (1998)

Although supporters of the HRA argue that it simply brings into British law those rights previously available to British citizens under the ECHR, the application of these guarantees since the HRA came into force has given cause for concern.

A particular bone of contention has been the extent to which the Act has been used by those who engender little public sympathy, specifically criminals and foreign nationals facing deportation. The case of the Afghan hijackers in 2006 provides a clear illustration of this point. Originally arrested and charged with a range of offences in connection with the hijacking of a passenger airliner, nine Afghans who were said to have fled from the Taliban were ultimately allowed to remain in the UK and seek employment after the government was found to have denied them the rights they were entitled to under the HRA.

Politicians v judges

The HRA has seen senior UK judges coming into conflict with government ministers on a more regular basis than was previously the case, an inevitable consequence of an emergent rights culture. The anti-terror legislation that came in the wake of the attacks on 9/11 and 7/7 has raised serious questions regarding the proper relationship between the judiciary and politicians. However, the key function of an independent judiciary is to protect citizens from a government that seeks to erode their rights and encroach upon their freedoms — whatever the circumstances.

This observation is particularly true in respect of the judicial criticism of the use of the indefinite detention without trial of terrorist suspects under the Anti-terrorism, Crime and Security Act (2001) and the imposition of control orders under the Prevention of Terrorism Act (2005). Both measures struck at the heart of the presumption of innocence, the right to a free and fair trial, and the freedom from arbitrary arrest and imprisonment.

Ultimately, of course, the government is not required to give way under pressure from judges. Declarations of incompatibility issued under the HRA only invite Parliament to reconsider its position. As we have seen, the UK government can also apply to derogate some of the guarantees enshrined in the ECHR in times of national emergency.

The case for replacing the Human Rights Act with a UK Bill of Rights is, therefore, far from overwhelming.

Should the UK replace the HRA with a new Bill of Rights?

Yes:

- The HRA has placed too much power into the hands of senior judges, thus challenging the doctrine of parliamentary sovereignty and tying the hands of senior politicians.
- The HRA has faced widespread criticism in the press and does not enjoy the confidence of the general public.
- A UK Bill of Rights would protect rights in a manner more in keeping with our common law traditions.

No:

- Repeal of the HRA would not remove the UK's obligations under the ECHR, it would just put power back into the hands of the ECtHR in Strasbourg.
- Cherry-picking certain rights to include in this new Bill of Rights would serve only to undermine other rights that were no longer formally enshrined.
- In the absence of a codified constitution, there is no way of effectively entrenching any new Bill of Rights.

Knowledge check 8

Explain the term 'entrenchment' in the context of proposals to introduce a new UK Bill of Rights.

Summary

After studying this topic you should be able to:

- Define the term 'constitution' and understand how it relates to the concepts of 'the state' and 'limited government'.
- Distinguish between 'codified' and 'uncodified' constitutions and understand their origins.
- Understand the concept of 'fundamental law' and relate it to the idea of entrenchment.
- Demonstrate knowledge and understanding of the main sources and principles of the UK Constitution.
- Understand the particular importance of statute law and parliamentary sovereignty.
- Identify, analyse and evaluate recent constitutional reforms.
- Show an understanding of the kinds of rights that are protected in the UK and the means by which such protection is achieved.
- Evaluate the Human Rights Act (1998) and the Freedom of Information Act (2000) and discuss the case for and against drafting a new UK Bill of Rights.

■ The structure and role of Parliament

Parliament performs three main functions:

1 Scrutiny: both houses are responsible for holding the government to account. Parliamentary committees in both houses scrutinise the government's performance and the Commons has the ultimate power to remove a government through a vote of no confidence.

2 Representation: a primary function of Parliament is to act as the nation's representative assembly. While the Commons represents the specific interests and constituencies and grievances of constituents, the Lords can be seen to represent a wide range of causes and other interests.

3 Legislation: both houses are involved in the passage of legislation. The vast majority of bills are government-backed and originate in the Commons; however, the expertise in the House of Lords improves and amends most legislation and can delay it for up to a year.

Other functions include:

■ Both houses provide a forum for debating and voting on key issues and in doing so act as a vital training and recruiting ground for future ministerial positions.

■ The democratically elected Commons legitimises government activity by holding to account and/or supporting the government's policies and legislative proposals.

Scrutiny of the executive and how effective such scrutiny is in practice

A committee-based institution?

There are several ways that Parliament can scrutinise the work of the **executive** or government, thereby holding it to account. One of the most prominent is through the work of committees.

The growing complexity of political and legislative activity, alongside reforms to the role and remit of committees, has seen a significant shift towards Parliament becoming a committee-based institution, meaning that much of its most productive work takes place away from its main chambers.

Select committees

Select committees play a vital role in examining the performance of the government. Departmental select committees scrutinise each department of state while others, such as the Public Accounts Committee, have a more general brief.

■ The **Public Accounts Committee** scrutinises all aspects of government expenditure, seeking to highlight wastefulness and inefficiency. The committee drew attention to NHS spending and has highlighted many activities of non-parliamentary bodies, especially large businesses considered to be paying too little corporation tax.

> **Exam tip**
>
> Ensure that you can identify the main roles of Parliament and evaluate, with examples, the extent to which they are performed effectively.

> **Executive** Refers to all those charged with executing and administering laws passed by the government — the prime minister, cabinet, other senior government ministers and civil servants.

- The **Commons Liaison Committee** is made up of the chairs of all departmental select committees and since 2002 requires the prime minister, by convention, to appear before it twice a year. In December 2016 prime minister Theresa May was quizzed by the committee over Parliament's role in negotiations to leave the EU.

Established in the 1970s and boosted by Margaret Thatcher in 1979, select committees are now a prominent part of Parliament's activities. Successive reports on them — Norton (2000), Newton (2001) and the Wright reforms following the 2010 general election — have succeeded in strengthening the powers of select committees and in widening their remit. A much-cited report by University College London (UCL) reviewed the policy recommendations made by seven of the most prominent select committees between 1997 and 2010, concluding that the government had acted on 44% of policy recommendations.

However, the inability of select committees to compel the government to comply with their recommendations, or to force people from outside Parliament to attend and to testify, is seen as a significant weakness. In addition, as evidenced by the UCL report, well over half of all select committee recommendations are ignored.

Knowledge check 9

What are the Wright reforms? Outline two key changes that they brought in.

Public bill committees

All legislation passes through a committee stage when a group of MPs (usually 15–25 members), made up in proportion to the party make-up of the Commons, evaluates a bill clause by clause. These are not permanent committees but are set up while the legislation is passing through Parliament — considering the legislation following its second reading — and disbanded when work is complete.

These legislative committees often invite written evidence from interested parties in efforts to enhance the legislation and clarify any imprecise aspects. Critics of the effectiveness of public bill committees point to the power of the government party to both curtail debate (by using a guillotine motion) and 'whip' committee members to follow party guidelines. In addition, any committee amendments can be ignored at the bill's next reading in Parliament.

Exam tip

Remember that public bill committees in the Commons consider legislation only after its second reading, by which stage the main provisions and principles of any bill are firmly established.

Committees in the House of Lords

A range of committees operates within the House of Lords, scrutinising proposed laws and government activity, just as they do in the Commons. Despite its unelected status, the expertise and experience within the House of Lords can present a formidable check on executive power. In the 2014/15 parliamentary session, the Lords defeated the Commons 11 times, usually on issues involving the protection of vulnerable groups such as children or overseas workers.

Examples of executive scrutiny by committees in the Lords include:
- legislation: in the 2015/16 session, the Lords examined 43 bills; at the committee stage, line-by-line scrutiny takes place
- scrutiny: House of Lords select committees are usually made up of around 12 members meeting to consider public policy and government action; their findings are published and debated in the chamber. Examples of Lords select committees include the Science and Technology Committee and the Social Mobility Committee

- inquiry: some committees take the form of an inquiry into a specific area — recent inquiries have investigated the UK housing market, and the sustainability of Channel 4.

Exam tip

Research the most recent examples of government defeats within the Lords to ensure that your answers are up to date.

Comparison

Committees in the UK and the USA

It is often argued that committees within the UK Parliament are significantly weaker than their American counterparts. Committees in the USA are regarded as the real 'powerhouses' in Congress, with huge financial and personnel resources to research issues in substantial depth and with greatly enhanced legal powers to compel witnesses to testify before them.

Despite this unfavourable comparison, committees in the Commons have grown in stature and relevance in recent decades and play a valuable role in scrutinising the government and examining legislation.

Prime Minister's Questions (PMQs) and ministers' questions

Prime Minister's Questions takes place every Wednesday for 30 minutes when Parliament is in session. It is an opportunity for any MP to question the prime minister on the performance of the government and on issues of national and international importance. Critics often refer to PMQs as an overly aggressive and unproductive 'bear pit', little more than 'political theatre', rather than an opportunity for effective scrutiny of the prime minister or the government. Most members of the public see only a tiny fraction of PMQs on news programmes, encouraging the main participants to favour short, media-friendly sound bites over detailed scrutiny.

However, PMQs remains a widely celebrated example of parliamentary scrutiny at the highest level, and the prospect of a question on any aspect of the government's performance requires prime ministers to have as full and frank a knowledge of all the relevant issues and matters of state as possible.

Additionally, all government ministers are required to face similar questions in Parliament, enabling individual MPs to raise issues of concern, often on behalf of affected constituents.

Early day motions, e-petitions and the 'vote of no-confidence'

There are a number of practical devices and procedures that Parliament as a whole and individual MPs can utilise to scrutinise the executive or hold it to account:

- **Early day motions** (EDMs) are debates proposed by individual MPs, and supported by others, to raise awareness of a wide range of issues. While there is no time to

Parliamentary session The parliamentary year that begins with the Queen's Speech in November.

Knowledge check 10

Outline an argument for and an argument against PMQs as an effective method of executive scrutiny.

Early day motion A form of parliamentary petition where an MP tables a bill for debate in the Commons, to which other MPs can add their names.

debate more than a handful of EDMs in each parliamentary session, it is a device used to highlight concerns and to raise awareness of issues affecting constituents.

■ Since August 2011, Commons debates can be prompted by e-petitions that gather more than 100,000 signatures. Between 2011 and 2015, 32 e-petition-prompted debates took place, ranging from fuel tax to the treatment of domestic pets, with a small number prompting government action. In response to a petition signed by more than 155,000 people, in November 2015 MPs debated the introduction of a 'sugar tax'. The debate drew a sizable Commons gathering, but in spite of a vote overwhelmingly in favour, minister Jane Ellison told those assembled that the government had 'no plans' to introduce a tax within its obesity strategy. However, the then Chancellor George Osborne, in his March 2016 budget, announced a levy on soft drinks manufacturers, linked to the amount of sugary drinks they sell. It was a policy very much like the 'sugar tax' which had seen such significant petition-backed public support just the previous year.

■ A formal vote or motion of no-confidence can, if lost by the government of the day, prompt the dissolution of Parliament and a general election. The prospect of a no-confidence motion is usually remote for a government with a substantial Commons majority, but cooperation between opposition parties can be problematic for minority administrations or governments with slender majorities. Fixed-term parliaments may well have further removed the possibility of being toppled by a no-confidence motion.

The role of the Opposition

By convention, Her Majesty's Opposition is formed by the second largest party in the House of Commons, with its leader becoming the leader of the Opposition. An effective Opposition can robustly oppose government policies, present coherent alternatives and occasionally gather enough support, involving minor parties and disaffected members on the government's backbenches, to defeat the government. Between 2010 and 2016 there were nine government defeats on votes ranging from proposed intervention in the Syrian War to the under-occupancy penalty (or 'bedroom tax').

The Opposition performs several functions:

■ Organisation of Opposition Days: the vast majority of the parliamentary calendar is dictated by the government, but 20 days are set aside as Opposition Days; 17 of these are controlled by the Official Opposition, 3 are organised by the 'third party'. While enacting legislation on these days is not practically possible, highlighting unpopular government policies and presenting coherent alternatives is the norm.
  – In the 2015/16 parliamentary session, Labour debated a range of issues during its Opposition Days, including EU membership (prior to the referendum vote), NHS funding and the Paris Agreement on climate change.
  – In the same session the SNP used some of its allocated Opposition Days to debate Trident renewal and the humanitarian crisis in the Mediterranean.

■ The Leader of the Opposition is seen as a prime minister in waiting, leading a 'shadow' cabinet that represents a 'government in waiting'. The 30-minute weekly interrogation of the prime minister is the most prominent of the Opposition's functions. It is especially incumbent on the Leader of the Opposition to rally their party and expose government ineffectiveness.

Exam tip

It is wise not to overstate the prospect of a successful no-confidence motion. The 2010–15 coalition government survived without a scare; the most recent example of a government being toppled by one was back in 1979.

Knowledge check 11

Explain why it is rare for a government to lose a vote of no-confidence.

Exam tip

The Official Opposition and smaller opposition parties receive public money to ensure that they can operate effectively.

Exam tip

Research online for some strong recent examples of how opposition parties have used their Opposition Days to scrutinise the executive.

Knowledge check 12

Outline two ways that Parliament can scrutinise the government.

Parliamentary debate and the legislative process

The principles of parliamentary sovereignty and parliamentary government mean that Parliament is at the centre of political activity in the UK.

- Parliamentary sovereignty is one of A.V. Dicey's twin pillars of the British constitution, along with the rule of law. This principle dictates that there is no higher authority than Parliament and that Parliament can make and unmake any law at will.
- The centrality of Parliament within the UK political system means that all legislation has to be passed by Parliament. However, the devolution of primary legislative powers to regional assemblies in Scotland and Wales is seen to have eroded this principle.
- In theory, all political power emanates from Parliament: the government is drawn from Parliament, the leader of the largest party in the House of Commons becomes the prime minister, and all ministers within the government are accountable to Parliament.

The structure of the UK Parliament is bicameral. Many parliamentary functions are performed by both the Commons and the Lords. For example, both houses are involved in approving and amending legislation, in scrutinising government activity and in debating major political issues. Some functions are not performed by both Houses. For example, only MPs within the House of Commons represent and are accountable to constituents; peers within the House of Lords are electorally accountable to no one.

Bicameralism

A legislature comprising two chambers is said to be bicameral and most modern democracies have two legislative chambers. While the 'lower' house is usually democratically elected and often the dominant chamber, the composition of 'upper' houses vary — some are directly elected (e.g. the Senate in the US Congress), while others are indirectly elected or selected.

Advantages of bicameralism:

- A second chamber can provide greater checks and balances on government power and allow for the enhanced revision of legislation.
- A chamber that is less partisan or less sensitive to the immediate prospect of an election can represent different interests (e.g. those of disadvantaged groups or minorities) and consider the longer-term impact of actions and legislation.

Disadvantages of bicameralism:

- If the two chambers or houses are in conflict, legislative **gridlock** can occur, leading to inaction or excessive delay.
- An indirectly elected upper house can either be increasingly marginalised by or block the agenda of a democratically elected lower house.

Knowledge check 13

Explain briefly the system of checks and balances.

Exam tip

Research and include some brief examples of second chambers and the ways in which they are elected or selected, allowing you to make comparisons with the UK.

Gridlock Most commonly associated with the US system of government where a complete separation of powers between executive and legislature can lead to stalemate.

> **Comparison**
>
> ### Bicameralism in the UK and the USA
> The relationship between the two houses within the UK Parliament is referred to as asymmetric bicameralism, highlighting the significantly greater power possessed by the Commons over the Lords. In the USA, the relationship is referred to as balanced bicameralism, emphasising that legislative power between the House of Representatives and the Senate is largely co-equal.

The House of Commons

The House of Commons is the democratically elected chamber within the British Parliament. Despite its being known as the lower chamber, the vast majority of the important work of Parliament originates and is resolved within the House of Commons.

- The Commons consists of 650 MPs, each representing a constituency — a geographic area with roughly 70,000 voters.
- The largest party in the Commons following a general election forms the government or is the leading partner in a coalition government.
- Leading figures in government or in the shadow cabinet are known as frontbenchers; other MPs are known as backbenchers.
- Much of the work of the Commons takes place within committees:
  - Departmental and other select committees scrutinise government departments, question civil servants and other public figures, and write wide-ranging reports.
  - **Public bill committees** are legislative committees that review and amend legislation during its passage through Parliament.
- The government controls much of the parliamentary agenda and **whips** within main parties ensure party MPs are aware of votes taking place, seeking to maintain party discipline when they do.
- The death or resignation of an individual MP triggers a by-election to find a replacement.

Public bill committees Set up to scrutinise legislation. For example, the committee that oversaw the government's 2016 Finance Bill made a range of amendments, including those to combat tax avoidance.

Whips As well as maintaining party discipline, party whips ensure that channels of communication between backbench and frontbench MPs are effective.

The House of Lords

The House of Lords is the unelected chamber within the UK's bicameral parliament. It is made up of a range of different types of peers: some hold their titles by hereditary right, others are appointed for the duration of their lifetime; some are strongly affiliated to a political party while others consider themselves to be non-partisan.

Despite being referred to as the 'upper house', in keeping with other parliamentary systems the powers of the Lords are far less substantial than those of the electorally accountable House of Commons. However, one of the main roles of the Lords is to use its expertise to revise government legislation. Although restricted by the Parliament Acts of 1911 and 1949 to a maximum delay of one year (or one month for financial bills), the Lords has used its power of delay to extract important legislative concessions, especially in safeguarding civil liberties in recent years.

The House of Lords is made up of:

- **Lords Temporal**: currently numbering around 700 and known widely as 'life peers'. Following the Life Peerages Act (1958), life peers are appointed by the monarch on the advice of the prime minister and after being scrutinised by the House of Lords Appointments Commission. Life peers now make up the vast majority of the members of the House of Lords.
- **Hereditary peers** (Lords who inherit their titles): currently numbering 92, these are still permitted to sit in the Lords chamber on an interim basis following a compromise that enabled the House of Lords Act (1999) to pass.
- **Lords Spiritual**: 26 archbishops and bishops of the Church of England
- **crossbenchers**: usually around 200 peers who are not affiliated to any party.

Table 4 The Commons and Lords by party affiliation*

Party	House of Commons	House of Lords
Conservative	317	254
Labour	262	201
Nationalist parties	57	8
Liberal Democrat	12	101
Green Party	1	1
Other	1	37
Crossbenchers	n/a	177
Lords Spiritual	n/a	25
Total	650	804

* Summer 2017

Debate

One of the central roles of Parliament is the very public process of debating policies, issues and especially legislation as it passes through Parliament. This happens in a number of ways:

- Ministers make statements to Parliament on significant issues and these are followed by debate.
- Half-hour adjournment debates at the end of each day allow MPs the opportunity to address or raise issues of importance.
- While most debates are poorly attended, notable ones — such as the commitment of troops to the Syrian War in 2013 — are marked by impassioned and high-quality contributions from across the house.
- The Backbench Business Committee, created in 2011, determines the agenda for debate on one day a week. In October 2016 Conservative and SNP MPs united to trigger a debate on benefit cuts through the Backbench Business Committee.

Knowledge check 14

What are departmental select committees? Use examples in your answer.

Knowledge check 15

Explain why some hereditary peers survived the 1999 House of Lords Act.

Crossbencher A peer who does not 'take the whip' (align to) any political party. Crossbenchers sit on the benches positioned at right angles to the main frontbenches in the Lords.

Exam tip

When required to evaluate Parliament, be sure to refer to both Houses — the Commons and the Lords — depending upon the specific angle of the question.

Knowledge check 16

Using the information in both the Constitution and Parliament topics, explain briefly the significance of the Fixed-term Parliaments Act.

Parliamentary privilege

A key element of the process of parliamentary debate and deliberation is the legal immunity enjoyed by MPs in both houses. Known as 'parliamentary privilege', this means that MPs can carry out their parliamentary duties without interference or concern about prosecution. For example, MPs have revealed information that is subject to court injunctions. However, as the **expenses scandal** demonstrated, this does not place MPs above the law.

The legislative process

The British Parliament is the UK's sovereign legislative body, meaning that only it has the power to pass UK-wide legislation. This is complicated by the process of devolution, which has seen regional bodies take responsibility for legislating in their areas, and also by the surrendering of areas of sovereignty — such as agriculture, health and safety, and consumer protection — to the European Union, for the duration of the UK's membership.

Two types of bills exist:

- Public bills are either government bills (usually contained within a manifesto, supported by the government and invariably passed into law) or Private Members' bills (originating with individual MPs, they are usually doomed to fail unless receiving government backing).
- Private bills are specific and affect certain individuals or organisations and not the general public.

The passage of legislation is as follows:

- First reading: introduction and timetabling.
- Second reading: ministerial explanation, debate and vote.
- Committee stage: scrutiny by public bill committee, amendments proposed as appropriate.
- Third reading: voting on amendments, vote.
- Lords stage: similar process to the Commons with any amendments voted on by the Commons.
- Royal assent: the signing of the Act into law by the monarch.

Speeding up the legislative process

Of course, while some bills sail through each stage, others are beset by difficulties and delays. Tactics and powers available to the government to speed up the process include:

- using whipped votes in the committee stage to limit the success of Opposition-backed amendments
- using guillotine motions to curtail debate, especially in the committee stage
- making concessions to unsupportive backbenchers or to limit the Lords' power of delay of up to a year
- threatening or using the Parliament Act to bypass the Lords.

Expenses scandal In order to cover the cost of running offices, hiring assistants and maintaining a 'second' home in London, MPs can claim significant expenses. The system was revamped after the 2009 MPs' expenses scandal, which resulted in hundreds of MPs having to return money and four being jailed.

Exam tip

While the majority of Private Members' bills fail through lack of support, some notable ones have succeeded. Include some examples and statistics of PMBs where appropriate.

Knowledge check 17

Outline and explain the term 'guillotine motion'.

Theories of representation — Burkean, delegate, mandate theories

Trustees and delegates

Representation is described as a relationship between individuals, where one person or group acts, debates and votes on behalf of another. Edmund Burke (1729–97) clarified what came to be known as 'Burkean representation' by explaining that 'your representative owes you not his industry alone, but his judgement; and he betrays instead of serving you, if he sacrifices to your opinion'.

For Burke, therefore, representatives should be considered to be **trustees**, using their judgement to act for the common and national good as well as in the interests of their constituents.

Delegates, meanwhile, are said to act on behalf of a group or organisation and are rarely allowed to stray from clear expectations.

Representation and the Commons

There are two elements to any analysis of Parliament's representative function. Does the composition of Parliament resemble the wider population of the UK (**resemblance theory**)? And does it matter?

According to theories of representation, an effective elected assembly should be a 'descriptive' representation of the society from which it is drawn. Sometimes referred to as a 'microcosm', this description should mirror the proportional size of all major social groups. While the Commons may well have become much more descriptively representative in recent decades, it is *not* representative of the population of the UK in several key areas:

- Gender: the representation of women has improved significantly but still only 29% of MPs elected in 2015 were women (up from 22% in 2010). At the time of writing there were 191 female MPs, a record high.
- Age: the average age of MPs elected in 2015 was 51. However, the average age of those elected for the first time in 2015 was 44. Ages ranged among the whole 2015 cohort from the oldest MP, Sir Gerald Kaufman (Father of the House, born in 1930 and an MP since 1970), to the youngest at 20 years old, Mhairi Black (SNP).
- Ethnicity: the 2015 general election returned 41 MPs from ethnic minorities (6%) — up from 27 in 2010. Twenty-five of the 27 ethnic minority candidates elected in 2010 retained their seats. Despite this, the Commons remains a disproportionately white/Christian chamber.
- Socio-economic status: in 2015 more than nine out of ten MPs in the Commons had a university education, and 26% of them had attended Oxford or Cambridge universities. More than a third of MPs in the Commons went to fee-paying schools, compared with just 7% of the population.

While the unrepresentative nature of the Commons means that it stands accused of lacking a legitimate **mandate**, the reality is that there will always be many constituents represented by people who are unlike themselves. MPs are 'entrusted' to represent all constituents, regardless of ethnicity, faith or gender, and many work tirelessly to further the interests of minorities and disadvantaged groups within their constituencies.

Trustee Has no formal responsibility for the interests of others but, having been 'entrusted' with a particular responsibility, their actions should be responsible and accountable.

Delegate Has the authorisation to act on behalf of others, while being bound by clear instructions.

Resemblance theory Holds that in order to represent the values, beliefs and concerns of the population, an elected legislature should accurately reflect its constituent parts.

Knowledge check 18

Identify two ways in which the composition of the Commons has changed in recent years.

Mandate The authority of a democratically elected government to carry into law the policies contained within its pre-election manifesto.

Many MPs seek innovative ways to engage with their constituents. Opportunities for the public to examine the performance of their elected representatives or voice their opinions have never been greater. Nevertheless, the Scottish Parliament, for example, enjoys close to a 50/50 gender balance, as do many other modern democratic assemblies. The question remains whether the House of Commons is able to understand and effectively represent a society that it does not accurately resemble.

Representation and the Lords

The House of Lords experienced radical change following the House of Lords Act (1999) when all but 92 hereditary peers were removed from the chamber. The previous 'in-built Tory majority' was eradicated since the vast majority of hereditary peers were Conservative (471 to Labour's 179). The large number of Labour life peers appointed after 1999 redressed the party balance. At the time of writing, the two main parties still dominate the Lords with more than 460 peers between them (Conservatives 255; Labour 206). However, 182 peers consider themselves to be crossbenchers with no discernible party loyalty.

Despite being unelected and unrepresentative (there are nearly three times the number of male life peers to female life peers), the Lords is praised for its inclusion of experts in the fields of human rights, science, business and innovation, health and education and the armed forces. However, it is still seen as being socially elite and lacks any form of accountability.

The appointment of life peers

The Life Peerages Act (1958) was designed to revive an upper house seen as being out of touch with a rapidly changing society. Although appointments are made by the monarch, the prime minister — on the advice of the House of Lords Appointments Commission — has a great deal of autonomy. The process has been the subject of controversy as several prime ministers have made peerages specifically to include members of their governments (Gordon Brown ennobled Peter Mandelson in 2009 and made him Secretary of State for Business, Innovation and Skills) while others have ennobled major party donors amidst accusations of cronyism.

The roles and influence of MPs and peers

How effective are backbench MPs?

MPs perform a huge range of representative functions, from local constituency activities (e.g. opposing proposals such as factory closures or planning developments) to work within Parliament (e.g. supporting party policies on a range of issues or scrutinising government activities in committees). When evaluating the effectiveness of MPs, consider the following areas:

- Much backbench impact occurs at committee level — while statistics point to the fact that many committee amendments are later defeated in the chamber, a large number are included to refine legislation. However, backbench MPs are frequently involved at a far earlier stage: shaping legislation prior to its passage through Parliament.
- The threat of a backbench rebellion is often enough to dissuade governments from introducing unpopular legislation. Backbenchers can mobilise this threat to extract key concessions.

Exam tip

Having a clear understanding of resemblance theory will be useful in tackling wider questions on representation in topics covering electoral systems.

Exam tip

Research and use up-to-date examples of recently appointed life peers using their expertise to contribute positively to the parliamentary process.

Cronyism The practice of awarding roles and rewards to friends or supportive individuals regardless of their qualifications or abilities.

Exam tip

Research Professor Philip Cowley's 'Revolts' website (revolts.co.uk/) for analysis of recent backbench rebellions.

■ Select committee inquiries allow backbench MPs the chance to examine key witnesses, including senior officials and public or prominent figures. In 2016 the Business, Innovation and Skills Committee questioned Mike Ashley, owner of Sports Direct.

■ Prime Minister's Questions allows backbench MPs to publicly cross-examine the prime minister on a regular basis, something rarely seen in other democracies.

How have recent reforms enhanced the power of MPs?

Two main reforms have made a significant impact on the power of MPs to hold governments to account.

1 Changes to select committees:
   – Elections of the committee chair now take place by secret ballot, negating government pressure on MPs to select a favoured candidate.
   – Chairs are paid an additional salary, which has served to make them more independently minded.
   – Select committees have increasingly sought to widen their remits, producing hard-hitting reports on major cross-departmental issues such as poverty, social care and inequality.

2 The Backbench Business Committee:
   – Created in 2010, the Backbench Business Committee controls the parliamentary agenda on 35 days a year (approximately one day per week).
   – The chair must be a member of the Opposition and members are voted in using proportional electoral systems.
   – Many recent and significant political events have been prioritised by the Backbench Business Committee, such as the 2012 reopening of the investigation into the Hillsborough disaster.

The less partisan character of the House of Lords ensures that it is often seen as a place of genuine debate and effective, informed criticism of government activity. The strength of having experts involved in the legislative process is widely acknowledged and this only serves to enhance the legitimacy of the laws generated. In times of weak Commons opposition, such as 1997–2005, the Lords can be a potent check on government power.

How powerful are peers?

The most significant power of peers is their ability to delay the passage of legislation by up to a year. While the Lords cannot delay 'money bills', they can frequently delay important government policy and legislation by defeating it, usually in a bid to force a change.

There is no doubt that changes to the composition of the Lords since the abolition of most hereditary peers have enhanced both its legitimacy and its assertiveness. The inclusion — as life peers — of experts or experienced practitioners in fields such as healthcare, policing, education, human rights, business and defence have added significantly to the ability of the Lords to enhance and enrich the debate within it and the legislation that passes through it. In addition, the Lords has proved itself to be a formidable opponent of hastily drawn-up government legislation.

Money bills Bills that the Speaker has categorised as entirely to do with money (e.g. the Budget) are not opposed by the Lords under the provisions of the Parliament Acts (1911 and 1949).

In the 2014/15 parliamentary session, the House of Lords defeated the government 11 times. Two examples are:

- October 2014: the Lords rejected the Criminal Justice and Courts Bill as it did not provide adequate protection for children under the age of 15.
- February 2015: the Lords insisted on a legislative amendment to the Modern Slavery Bill to give greater protection to overseas domestic workers.

What factors limit the power of peers?

In response to Lords resistance to the 1909 Liberal Budget, the Parliament Act of 1911 transformed the power of the Lords by replacing their legislative veto with a two-year delay and preventing them from debating and voting on money bills.

The Salisbury Convention, dating from 1945, ensured that the Lords would not vote against legislation contained in a government's manifesto.

The Parliament Act of 1949 reduced the power of delay to one year. However, it has been used on only four occasions since.

The process of Lords reform

There have been three distinct phases in the process of reform to the House of Lords:

- The House of Lords Act (1999): the frustrations of the Labour Party in opposition, together with an acknowledgement that with more than 1,300 members the Lords was cumbersome and ineffective, saw the removal of all but 92 hereditary peers in a 'transitional house', a key element of New Labour's constitutional reforms.
- Reform suspended (1999–2010): commissions and White Papers detailing various proportions of elected and appointed peers led to vague Labour manifesto commitments in 2001 and 2005, subsequent free votes in the Commons and the Lords, but no further progress in settling the size and nature of the second chamber.
- Reform stalled (2010–present): parliamentary reform featured high on the Liberal Democrat agenda and Lords reform was a bargaining chip in the original coalition agreement in 2010. Conservative support for a fully elected second chamber was not forthcoming and Nick Clegg's 2012 proposals were abandoned amidst claims that the Conservatives had 'broken the coalition contract' in not supporting it.

Interactions of Parliament and other branches of government

Parliament and the executive: 'elective dictatorship'?

A combination of a lack of separation of powers which allows the executive to be part of the legislature, a majoritarian electoral system that usually presents governments with over-large majorities, and an uncodified constitution whereby no clear understanding of the distribution of power exists means it is hardly surprising that the executive is able to dominate Parliament. Practically speaking, there are two explanations for this domination:

- Patronage, party loyalty and 'career politicians': the power of the prime minister to distribute responsibilities, together with a general acceptance that the winning of a general election gives the government a mandate to carry out its legislative programme, is often enough to ensure that resistance is limited. Add to this the

Exam tip

Research online for the latest proposals for Lords reform.

Career politicians Some prominent politicians are criticised for having little or no professional experience outside of politics. The improvement in working hours, salaries and allowances in recent years has enhanced the attractiveness of the job of an MP.

narrow professional experience of many politicians and a culture of faithfully serving the party prevails.

■ The power and influence of the whips: where further persuasion is required, the organisational role of party whips can be significant. There is an expectation that the party rank-and-file vote the way of their leaders and the 'carrot and stick' approach of the whips prevails. Government defeats are rare.

Parliamentary sovereignty or elective dictatorship?

Parliamentary sovereignty is identified as one of the twin pillars of the UK's Constitution. In theory, Parliament is supreme: it can make or abolish any law and is not bound by any other body, including previous parliaments.

In practice, however, commentators maintain that while legislative sovereignty remains with Parliament, on a day-to-day basis real power — political sovereignty — lies with the executive. The lack of a separation of powers allows the executive to dominate Parliament (all members of the executive are within the legislature) and the prevalence of large electoral majorities has prompted some — most notably Lord Hailsham in 1974 — to warn of 'elective dictatorship'.

The process of devolution of power to the regions, the surrendering of sovereignty to the European Union — for as long as the UK is a member, EU laws prevail where they conflict with UK laws — and the wider use of referendums have contributed to the erosion of parliamentary sovereignty.

Summary

After studying this topic you should be able to:

- Define the term 'parliament' along with key elements of the parliamentary process such as the Commons, the Lords and the Opposition.
- Demonstrate knowledge and understanding of the composition and the powers of the House of Commons and the House of Lords.
- Identify and explain the main roles and functions performed by Parliament — scrutiny, legislation, representation and debate.

- Be clear on the ways that Parliament can scrutinise the executive and how effective scrutiny is in practice.
- Understand the nature of parliamentary debate and the legislative process.
- Evaluate and analyse the effectiveness of the representative process, alongside different models of representation.
- Demonstrate an awareness of recent reforms to Parliament — the process of scrutiny, the role of individual MPs and the power of the Lords.

◼ The prime minister and cabinet

How policy is made

The prime minister and the core executive

The core executive is the focus for political power in the UK. It is the branch of government where the formulation and implementation of policy take place. Its high-profile nature — this is the location of the nation's political leaders and the origins of the policy and legislation that directly affect our lives — has led to much scrutiny and contention over how decisions are made and where power lies. The core executive contains a number of individuals and institution (see Table 5):

- The prime minister is the head of the government and chairs the cabinet.
- The cabinet is the decision-making body at the heart of government, usually comprising just over 20 of the most senior ministers (for example, the Home Secretary, the Foreign Secretary).
- Government ministers fill wider positions of responsibility within government departments (for example, the Financial Secretary to the Treasury, the Minister of State for Health).
- Government departments and civil servants are the main units of central government and the 'administrators' who work within (for example, the Department of Health is a ministerial department employing 2,160 civil servants).

Table 5 Examples of core executive roles

Position	Department	Description
Home Secretary	Home Office	Overall departmental responsibility for home affairs, including security and terrorism, legislation and spending
Foreign Secretary	Foreign & Commonwealth Office	Overall responsibility for UK foreign policy, intelligence policy and cyber security
Financial Secretary to the Treasury	UK Treasury	Supports the Chancellor of the Exchequer; oversight of the UK tax system, corporate and business taxation, European and international tax issues, HM Revenue & Customs
Minister of State for Health	Department of Health	Supports the Health Secretary; oversight of all aspects of hospital care, NHS performance and operations, the workforce, patient safety and maternity care

The changing relationships between the elements that comprise the core executive — the prime minister, ministers and civil servants — have long been the subject of debate and discussion. Factors that have blurred traditional lines of consultation and decision making include:

- the centralisation of power in the hands of the prime minister
- the growing complexity of government
- the rapid nature of political communication
- the rise of special advisers, independent of the permanent civil service.

Exam tip

When considering policy making, remember that the core executive is wider than just the prime minister and the cabinet.

The origins and evolution of the office of prime minister

The prime minister (or PM) is 'chief executive' of the government, holding an office that is largely based upon convention. When King George I (reigned 1714–27) became increasingly reluctant to attend and chair cabinet meetings, his **First Lord of the Treasury** deputised for him, in doing so becoming prime minister. While the steady growth in prime ministerial power since the early 1700s has not been entirely smooth, it has seen its holder assume significant, and in some cases unchecked, powers.

Notable early prime ministers included:

- Robert Walpole (in office 1721–42): George I's First Lord of the Treasury and generally held to be the UK's first prime minister
- William Pitt the Younger (1783–1801 and 1804–06): at the age of 24, Pitt the Younger remains the youngest ever prime minister
- Lord Liverpool (1812–27): oversaw the British victory in the Napoleonic Wars.

As the power of the monarch steadily declined to the ceremonial role recognisable today, the prime minister's role expanded to replace it. There is no fixed point at which the role of prime minister came into existence. Instead, powers have emerged or evolved in a number of ways:

- Assuming the royal prerogative: most prime ministerial powers were formerly exercised by the monarch. Known as 'royal prerogative' powers, these have been transferred to, or incorporated by, the prime minister over many years. They include controlling the armed forces, declaring war, signing treaties, appointing and dismissing ministers and organising the civil service.
- Assimilating powers by convention: in the absence of a codified constitution, certain powers have been assumed by convention — literally the process of doing things differently over time. Many important party and parliamentary practices, such as the expectation of party support via collective cabinet responsibility, have evolved to sustain the position of prime minister.

> **First Lord of the Treasury** 'Official' and historic title of the UK prime minister. The Second Lord of the Treasury is the Chancellor of the Exchequer.

> **Exam tip**
>
> Important concepts such as 'royal prerogative' and 'convention' appear in Topic 1 as well.

> **Knowledge check 20**
>
> Outline and explain the term 'collective cabinet responsibility'.

Comparison

The US president and the Constitution

One of the most significant principles of the US Constitution is the doctrine of the separation of powers. In its first three Articles, the Constitution sets out clearly the roles and responsibilities of the three branches of government and how they check and balance each other. Within Article II, the precise nature of executive power is detailed along with the limitations upon it. For example, the president has the power to sign treaties but only 'provided two thirds of the Senators ... concur'. Section 3 requires the president to 'give to the Congress information on the State of the Union' and Section 4 explains how and when a president 'shall be removed from Office on Impeachment'.

Who can become prime minister?

In essence, a PM needs to satisfy the following two requirements:

- Be a Member of Parliament: one of the prerequisites of becoming a prime minister is that the office holder is drawn from the Houses of Parliament. While early PMs were mainly drawn from the Lords, the extension of the franchise over the course of the 19th and early 20th centuries allowed for a far more diverse make-up of MPs, making controlling the more powerful Commons vital.

- Be the leader of the largest single party in the Commons: the most important element of prime ministerial power is his or her leadership of the largest party in the Commons. When a prime minister no longer holds such a role, their tenure is over. Margaret Thatcher was forced to resign as prime minister when she withdrew from the Conservative Party leadership contest in 1990; Theresa May automatically became prime minister when she became leader of the Conservative Party — and the largest Commons party — in 2016.

What are the main roles of the prime minister?

Unlike with the US president, there is no definitive list of roles or duties that explains or clarifies the office of the prime minister. Instead, commentators have attempted to set out or define the main characteristics of the role over time. Broadly speaking:

- the prime minister is the most senior minister within the government — the chief executive — and chairs the cabinet as **primus inter pares**
- the prime minister is head of the government and acts as head of state in most circumstances, providing national and international leadership
- as leader of the largest party in the Commons, the prime minister is chief legislator and controls much of the parliamentary agenda
- on the global stage, the prime minister represents the UK in world affairs, deploys the armed forces and is chief diplomat, with powers to sign international treaties.

What is the Prime Minister's Office?

The Prime Minister's Office supports the work of the prime minister from 10 Downing Street, the PM's official residence. It is headed by the prime minister's chief of staff and staffed by nearly 200 civil servants or political appointees. It comprises a collection of different offices that advise and support the prime minister. The main functions are:

- communication: with intense media focus on the prime minister, effective communication of government policy and prime ministerial positions is of paramount importance. Within the Prime Minister's Office is the Press Office and a range of other key communicators
- advice: the Prime Minister's Office is the coordinator of policy advice to enable the prime minister to set the strategic direction of the government and scrutinise the work of the departments of state. Over time and under different prime ministers, bodies such as the Private Office, the Political Unit, the Policy Unit and the Policy and Implementation Unit have been set up and reformed to coordinate policy making and implementation across government.

What are the main powers of the prime minister?

The British prime minister is head of the government, holding a post that has emerged and developed over several centuries. Several key responsibilities can be identified:

- Power of appointment ('hiring and firing'): the prime minister exercises the prerogative powers of appointment and dismissal of all senior members of the government — cabinet ministers, senior civil servants, peers, bishops and judges. Such patronage powers are extensive, command significant loyalty and enable the premier to promote and demote key allies or rivals.

Knowledge check 21

Outline and explain why leading the 'largest single party' is significant.

Primus inter pares
Latin term meaning 'first among equals': the theory that the prime minister is technically on the same level as his or her cabinet colleagues, operating within a collective decision-making body.

Knowledge check 22

What does the term 'head of state' mean?

Knowledge check 23

Outline and explain the role of the prime minister's chief of staff.

- Directing the government: setting policy objectives, short- and long-term strategic goals and determining the cabinet agenda are key prime ministerial responsibilities. While these are determined and achieved in conjunction with cabinet colleagues, the premier's personal role in policy making and agenda setting is formidable.
- Managing Parliament: the leadership of a majority party (or parties in times of coalition government) in the House of Commons is central to the prime minister's power. Control of the parliamentary timetable and expectations of party loyalty remain powerful prime ministerial tools. Fixed-term parliaments have largely removed the ultimate threat of dissolution.
- National and international leadership: in times of crisis the prime minister is expected to provide leadership — a role that is magnified in an era of intense media scrutiny. On a practical level, exercising the prerogative powers of waging war and signing treaties enhances the premier's standing and prestige.

What are the limits on the power of the prime minister?

The rise of the mass media and the centralisation of decision making have strengthened the British premier, but there remain several notable constraints on prime ministerial power — sometimes known as the 'six Ps':

Primus inter pares

This literally means 'first among equals', since an effective cabinet will balance wings or factions of the party and will contain senior figures who may not be natural allies of the prime minister. While prime ministers will want to reward those who have supported their rise to the top (such as George Osborne in 2010), ignoring or marginalising others can lead to difficulties. Three examples of the way that the action and behaviour of senior colleagues within the cabinet can limit the prime minister are:

- resignation: Margaret Thatcher may have lost the support of her party and the public, but it was the resignation of her Chancellor of the Exchequer, Geoffrey Howe, that finally led to her departure in 1990
- criticism: the highlighting of Tony Blair's cabinet 'control freakery' by Labour's Mo Mowlam was particularly damaging around the time of her departure from frontbench politics in 2001
- opposition: Michael Gove's frustration at being removed from the high-profile role of Education Secretary in 2014 is widely thought to have been behind his opposition to David Cameron in the 2016 EU referendum.

Party

Controlling the largest party in the Commons is a vital element of prime ministerial power. But while control of senior party colleagues is one thing, keeping backbenchers supportive and energised can be another entirely.

- Resentment on the backbenches prompted Anthony Meyer's 'stalking horse' leadership challenge of Thatcher in 1989, an act that revealed deep-seated opposition to the party leader from within.
- Sustained backbench criticism irreversibly undermined Gordon Brown's authority in the run-up to 2010.

Exam tip

Some prime ministerial powers are considered to be formal, others — such as the prime minister's ability to control party and Parliament — are informal and dependent on circumstances.

Knowledge check 24

Explain why the prime minister's patronage powers are so significant.

Parliament

The accountability function of Parliament requires the prime minister to face weekly questioning and be subject to the scrutiny of select committees. Legislative defeat is rare and can be particularly harmful to a PM's reputation when it occurs.

- David Cameron's first major Commons defeat — on EU spending in October 2012 — prompted a change of policy over Europe.
- An appearance before the Commons Liaison Committee in December 2016 prompted Theresa May to provide greater clarity on plans for parliamentary consultation over Britain's withdrawal from the EU.

People

Damaging opinion poll data, defeats in by-elections or disappointing local election performances can prove a significant check on prime ministerial power.

- The 'revolt of the shires' (local elections, May 2013) was said to be 'humbling' for David Cameron, the Conservative prime minister.
- After backing 'Remain' ahead of the EU referendum, Cameron felt compelled to resign his prime ministerial position after defeat.
- The 2017 general election proved disastrous for Theresa May's leadership: despite increasing the Tory vote (up 5.5% on 2015), the loss of 13 seats and the party's pre-election Commons majority were seen as an indictment of her uncharismatic and aloof campaign.

Personal qualities

Herbert Asquith's observation that 'the office of the prime minister is what its holder chooses and is able to make of it' remains highly relevant today. Charismatic leaders are often less likely to face challenges or defeats. Tony Blair's personal qualities enabled him to develop the prime ministerial role to 'presidential' status in the eyes of some commentators. Blair did not experience a Commons defeat in his first two terms, 1997–2005.

- John Major struggled to convince members of his own party and the public of his leadership qualities. Major faced a self-induced leadership challenge in 1995, a contest in which the then Conservative-backing *Sun* newspaper supported his opponent John Redwood under the headline 'Redwood versus Deadwood'. Major won the challenge but lost the 1997 general election in a Labour landslide.
- Gordon Brown struggled to convince both party and public of his leadership qualities. He was undermined by plots against his leadership for two years ahead of defeat in the 2010 general election.

Political circumstances

Healthy Commons majorities allow a premier to appear more effective and decisive. 'Events, dear boy. Events' was Harold Macmillan's explanation of the ebb and flow of prime ministerial power. Foreign wars or economic crises present unforeseen opportunities for a prime minister to either lead the way or appear incompetent.

- The 160-plus seat majority enjoyed by Tony Blair between 1997 and 2005 enabled him to ignore even significantly sized opposing factions within his party — those MPs often dubbed 'Old Labour'.

- A tale of two referendums: the successful devolution referendums in Scotland and Wales in 1997 emboldened Tony Blair to continue with his plan of devolution in London and elsewhere; the EU referendum 'defeat' for David Cameron saw him resign from prime ministerial office in 2016.
- Clearly the changed political and governing landscape after the 2017 general election has had a profound impact on Theresa May's ability to command the Commons and to steer legislation through it.

The powers and limits on the power of Prime ministers are listed in Table 6.

Table 6 Is the prime minister too powerful?

Powers	Limits
Appoints and dismisses ministers	Restricted by cabinet personnel
Controls cabinet agenda	Limited resources to control departments
Leads the largest party	Challenged by party
Enjoys high public profile	Blamed for policy failure

Has the British prime minister become 'presidential'?

Both Margaret Thatcher's and Tony Blair's leadership styles led many commentators to speculate that the prime minister had effectively become a 'president'. The argument rested upon a steady expansion in the role and according to Michael Foley's book *The Rise of the British Presidency* (1993) encompassed the cultivation of techniques such as 'spatial leadership' — the placing of the role above party political contests — and the 'Americanisation' of the office, with an apparent centralisation of decision making and an ever-increasing focus upon the personal role of the prime minister in political matters.

The real context of the debate is far more about perception than reality, since there are substantial differences between the largely unchecked prerogative powers wielded by a prime minister and the heavily circumscribed powers of a US president, limited by a codified constitution and operating within the clearly defined principle of the separation of powers. In addition, the characteristics of and challenges faced by recent prime ministers — Brown, Cameron and May — have to some extent laid to rest the notion that the UK is moving towards a 'presidential' model.

Arguments in favour of the prime minister becoming presidential include the following:
- The prerogative foreign policy powers of a prime minister are not dissimilar to the constitutional powers of the US president as commander-in-chief.
- The development of a dedicated prime ministerial department, the strengthening of the Cabinet Office (CO) and the wider use of special advisers give the appearance of a presidential-style **West Wing** or personal bureaucracy.
- The intense media focus upon the personality and character of the prime minister promotes the post-holder as an individual rather than a party leader.

Arguments against the prime minister becoming presidential include the following:
- The prime minister is not the head of state and the lack of a personal mandate through direct election is a key differentiator.
- The British Constitution makes no provision for a presidential-style leader and Parliament remains sovereign.
- The 'power' of a prime minister is largely down to personal and political circumstances — while Blair may have seemed 'presidential', Brown most certainly did not.

West Wing Synonymous with the section of the American White House which houses the president's closest aides and policy advisers.

Knowledge check 25

What is meant by the British prime minister becoming more 'presidential'?

The relationship between the prime minister and the cabinet

The organisation of the cabinet

Like the office of prime minister, the British cabinet has evolved over several centuries. It has been celebrated for its role in connecting the key elements of the governing process, which Walter Bagehot referred to as 'the hyphen which joins, a buckle which fastens the legislative part of the state to the executive part of the state'.

Cabinet organisation

- Modern cabinets comprise around 22–23 senior government figures (cabinet ministers) responsible for the key departments of state.
- The complexity of government decision making means that most decisions are ratified rather than discussed by the cabinet.
- Cabinet committees are where most decisions are made. Committees might comprise the prime minister and specific departmental ministers to cover key areas of foreign, home and economic affairs.
- The Cabinet Office (CO) is central to government decision making, coordinating the working of a vast array of government departments and personnel. The growth of the CO in recent years has provided the prime minister with the resources (around 2,000 staff) to be more active in departmental affairs.

Exam tip

Ensure that you have fully researched the decision-making bodies within government and are clear that many key decisions are not made at cabinet level.

Knowledge check 26

Explain the role of the Cabinet Office.

Focus: cabinet committees

These are subsets of the cabinet, usually chaired by the prime minister, with a particular policy area in mind (see Figure 1). It is often argued that the 'real business' of government takes place in cabinet committees, or in similarly focused groups such as 'implementation task forces' under David Cameron. Cabinet committees were reduced in number from 31 under Cameron to 21 under Theresa May, with many committees or subcommittees, such as those dealing with 'Troubled Families' and 'Health and Social Care', scrapped at this time.

While some cabinet committees are so well established they are virtually permanent — for example, the National Security Council — others are created according to the priorities of the prime minister. In 2016, the European Union Exit and Trade Committee was established to negotiate the UK's exit from the EU.

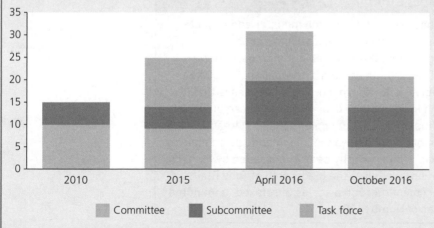

Figure 1 Number of cabinet committees by type, 2010 to October 2016

Source: Institute for Government analysis of Cabinet Office lists of cabinet committees

What are the main functions of the cabinet?

Traditionally, the cabinet has performed a number of key roles in the political system. In theory, the prime minister chairs the cabinet as primus inter pares, with all important decisions made at this level and members bound by collective responsibility to stand by them. The three main roles are:

- legitimising government decision making: the cabinet formalises government policy and is collectively bound by all government decisions (even ones taken in cabinet committees or elsewhere)
- resolving and coordinating policy: although the formulation of policy rarely takes place at cabinet level, the cabinet is the forum for ironing out departmental conflicts, determining the coherent presentation of policy and allocating appropriate funds
- crisis management: when emergencies arise, the cabinet becomes central. Health scares, economic crises and foreign wars ensure the cabinet's role as vital in providing political legitimacy and bolstering public confidence.

Prime minister and cabinet: who decides?
The decline of cabinet government?

In recent years, several factors have led to a decline in cabinet decision making:

- The complexity of government has reduced decision making at cabinet level — ministers cannot possibly grasp the detail of issues that are outside of their own departments.
- The prime minister's use of bilateral meetings and cabinet committees means that there are more focused and effective decision-making bodies than the cabinet.
- The growing status of the prime minister and his/her supporting infrastructure means that decisions made outside of the cabinet have increased status and legitimacy.
- The need to balance wings of the party within the cabinet means that some members of the decision-making body are unsympathetic to the prime minister's agenda. 'Inner cabinets', or 'kitchen cabinets', can provide far more productive forums for decision making.

Focus: informal decision-making forums

- Bilateral meetings are meetings between the prime minister and a single cabinet colleague to ensure that an effective decision is reached.
- An inner cabinet is a grouping of trusted senior cabinet members that meets on an informal basis. The strength of such a group is that it is likely to be more efficient and collegiate in its approach. The weakness is that it exchanges the formal decision making of the cabinet for an informality that can undermine cabinet government and upset senior cabinet colleagues.
- The term 'kitchen cabinet' further emphasises the informal decision making of some cabinet-level meetings. It has recently been superseded by the term 'sofa government', an accusation levelled at the leadership of Tony Blair, who frequently directed government through a series of relaxed, unminuted bilateral meetings on the sofas of Number 10.

The rise of prime ministerial government?

Some commentators have queried whether a time ever existed during which the cabinet was a genuinely collective decision-making body at the heart of government, though prime ministers such as Major and Cameron both took office promising to restore the cabinet to its central decision-making role.

In the second half of the twentieth century there is little doubt that cabinet power was substantially undermined by an increasingly dominant prime minister. But any suggestion of a linear flow of power misses the point. In reality, the decision-making process is complex and fluid. Different models exist that depend on factors such as the proximity of elections, the handling of crises and the authority or style of the prime minister:

- Prime ministerial government: key decisions are taken by the premier and his/her team of special advisers — or a 'kitchen cabinet' of senior figures — with cabinet ministers dealing on a departmental basis with their implementation.
- Differentiated prime ministerial control: in major departments of state (foreign, defence, economy), and especially matters of national security, the prime minister takes the lead, but in other areas, cabinet ministers are predominant.
- Departmental government: unless crisis intervenes, a minister's departmental expertise is unchallenged and coordinated at cabinet level by the prime minister.

> **Knowledge check 27**
>
> Outline and explain the term 'special advisers'.

The difference between individual and collective ministerial responsibility

Ministers are the most influential figures within the government. Senior ministers manage departments of state, are accountable for their performance and have a seat in cabinet. Civil servants and special advisers support senior and junior ministers in the process of policy formulation.

What is individual ministerial responsibility?

Individual ministerial responsibility is the principle that government ministers are singularly responsible for their own conduct and for the work of their departments. By convention, a minister should resign following an error or a failure to meet personal or departmental expectations. In addition, in a parliamentary system, ministers are accountable to Parliament for the performance of their departments.

However, the growing complexity of government and the rise of semi-autonomous agencies within most government departments means that ministers are no longer expected to be held personally responsible for operational matters handled by departmental officials, or decisions of which they had no knowledge. Recent years have seen a variety of reasons for ministerial resignations on the grounds of individual responsibility:

- Mistakes made by departmental officials: Sir Thomas Dugdale resigned in 1954 after errors made by officials within his department. His resignation is renowned as it led to the refining of expectations as detailed above.
- Policy failure: Britain's failure to acknowledge, or prepare for, the threat posed by Argentina prior to its invasion of the Falklands Islands led to the resignation of Foreign Secretary Lord Carrington in 1982 and two junior ministers.

> **Accountability**
> Individual ministerial responsibility provides a very good example of how the parliamentary system requires ministers to hold themselves accountable to regular oral and written questions from MPs and Parliament as a whole.

- Personal misconduct: a range of ministers have resigned after falling foul of principles set out in the Ministerial Code. David Laws resigned as Chief Secretary to the Treasury in 2010 after filing an incorrect expenses claim; Andrew Mitchell resigned as Chief Whip in 2012 after being accused of insulting a Downing Street policeman; Brooks Newmark resigned as Minister for Civil Society in 2014 after a newspaper alleged that he had sent explicit images.
- Political pressure: some ministers have resigned following sustained pressure over their competence to continue. Estelle Morris resigned as Education Secretary in 2001, explaining that she felt she was 'not up to the job'.

Knowledge check 28

What is the Ministerial Code?

What is collective ministerial responsibility?

Collective responsibility is a principle that underpins the effective functioning of the British government. It requires that:

- cabinet ministers are collectively bound by government decisions
- all members of the cabinet must support all government policy
- if a minister disagrees privately, he/she must defend publicly
- if a minister cannot maintain collective responsibility, he/she must resign their cabinet post.

The principle of collective responsibility rests on the notion that the cabinet is a united body — publicly at least — and that decisions reached around the cabinet table are binding on all of its members. In reality, the tensions and disagreements within a government mean that when ministers cannot uphold the principle, high-profile resignations are inevitable. Recent examples of resignations on grounds of collective ministerial responsibility include:

- Robin Cook resigned as Leader of the Commons in 2003 in opposition to the Iraq War
- Clare Short resigned as Secretary of State for International Development in 2003 over the UK's policy in post-war Iraq
- James Purnell resigned as Secretary of State for Work and Pensions in 2009 after criticising Gordon Brown's leadership
- Iain Duncan-Smith resigned as Secretary of State for Work and Pensions in 2016 in opposition to the government's budget cuts to disability benefits.

On occasions, the principle of collective responsibility is suspended to avoid ministerial resignations. This occurred during the two referendums on the UK's continued membership of the EU in 1975 and 2016.

Exam tip

Research the most up-to-date examples of ministerial resignations on grounds of individual and collective ministerial responsibility.

PM and cabinet: powers to dictate events and determine policy

Thatcher's government 1979–90

Margaret Thatcher is widely seen as one of the few British prime ministers to bring a distinct ideological shift to government. Her personal convictions — for a deregulated market economy, a reduction in trade union power and the privatisation of state-run industries — were instrumental in overturning the post-war consensus and reshaping Britain. Executive decision making was largely replaced by personal rule, and at cabinet meetings senior colleagues found themselves being briefed on decisions already made. Thatcher's style was to marginalise the cumbersome cabinet machinery in favour of policy making with trusted key advisers such as Keith Joseph and Alan Walters. This approach saw her determine policy in several prominent areas:

- Privatisation was a process that began with the successful sale of British Telecom and continued through most public utilities and industries, from British Steel to British Airways. It was driven by Thatcher's personal ideological commitments to a smaller state and greater competition, as well as revenue-raising priorities.
- The reduction of trade union power was another key plank in Thatcher's ideological platform. Her convictions saw the replacement of Employment Secretary James Prior with key ally Norman Tebbit in 1981 and the introduction of wide-ranging legislation to curb the power of the unions, culminating in an acrimonious victory over the mining unions in the mid-1980s.
- The introduction of the Poll Tax in 1990 has become a significant example of how strong prime ministers are able to dominate the decision-making and legislative process with disastrous results. Despite the misgivings of cabinet colleagues, the tax was pushed through Parliament and civil unrest ensued. Thatcher's high-handed manner frustrated most senior colleagues and she was forced to resign from office later the same year.
- Overseas it was the Falklands War that became a 'defining moment' in Thatcher's prime ministership. Within three days of the invasion on 2 April 1982, Thatcher had set up a small War Cabinet, through which the war was controlled, and despatched a naval taskforce to retake the islands. By mid-June Argentina had surrendered and Thatcher's decisive personal leadership, together with senior War Cabinet colleagues such as Deputy Prime Minister and Home Secretary Willie Whitelaw and Foreign Secretary Francis Pym, led to her being hailed a highly capable and committed war leader.

Major's government 1990–97

John Major's intentions for executive decision making had been all about collegiality upon his accession to Number 10, but his premiership was steadily overshadowed by a loss of authority and his slender government majority had been entirely overturned by 1997.

- Of the various areas that demonstrate decisive policy intervention, Major's engagement in the Northern Ireland peace process began soon after he took office in 1990. Major's personal involvement, together with his Northern Ireland Secretary Patrick Mayhew, led to the Downing Street Declaration of 1993 and an IRA ceasefire. It also paved the way for the historic Good Friday Agreement, signed soon after Major left office in 1998.
- Elsewhere, Major's commitment to 'keep Britain at the heart of Europe' was beset by difficulties and opposition from anti-EU senior colleagues. It led to his resignation, then re-election as party leader in 1995.

Blair's government 1997–2007

The Blair era was characterised by a dominant prime ministerial leadership style backed by the largest post-war Commons majority and largely shaped by bilateral meetings between the prime minister and key ministers of state. The result was rapid change in many areas, especially health, welfare, education and major constitutional reforms. However, such a style proved less robust when his popularity declined and Blair faced opposition or defeat in several key areas, most notably after the Iraq War in 2003.

Exam tip

Research some pre-1980s examples of executive policy making. The Wilson governments in the late 1960s and the 1970s provide good examples of unconsidered social and economic reforms, and the Heath government of the early 1970s took the UK into the EEC (the precursor to the EU).

Exam tip

Consider how the circumstances of John Major's premiership — especially his small Commons majority and the growing strength and cohesion of the opposition Labour Party — had an impact upon his government's ability to dictate policy and control events.

- Although Tony Blair had inherited the strong commitment to devolve power to the regions from his predecessor as Labour leader John Smith, reversing the centralisation of power which had reached its peak in the 1980s became something of a personal cause for Blair. Within two years of Blair becoming prime minister, regional assemblies had been created in Scotland, Wales, Northern Ireland and London.

Cameron's government 2010–16

David Cameron's prime ministership can be viewed only against a backdrop of coalition government and austerity. Coalition government required a much more collegial approach than his predecessors had needed, using bilateral meetings — with Deputy Prime Minister and coalition ally Nick Clegg — or meetings within a 'quad' that included George Osborne and Danny Alexander. Austerity provided the rationale to revive Thatcherite commitments to a small state, a free market economy and significant cuts to public spending. While coalition government undoubtedly curbed Cameron's capacity to determine the policy agenda, when he did secure a single-party majority government in 2015, his commitment to an in–out EU referendum proved to be his undoing.

- The 2015 Conservative manifesto pledge to hold a referendum on Britain's continued membership of the EU was realised in June 2016. It was described by *The Independent* as 'incredibly selfish recklessness', since Cameron's personal motive for holding the referendum was to close down an issue that had dogged many a previous Conservative leader. A further indictment of the prime minister's personal involvement in shaping events was revealed by the Foreign Affairs Select Committee in July 2016 discovering that Cameron had refused to allow the civil service to make plans for Brexit, a decision the committee described as 'an act of gross negligence'.

May's government 2016–

Theresa May entered office with extensive frontbench government experience, setting about strengthening the Prime Minister's Office and reorganising the cabinet system to ensure more direct control of key cabinet committees. However, while Brexit negotiations were set to dominate her initial years in office and likely to divide the Conservative Party, 2017 began with a 'humanitarian crisis' in hospital care and a funding crisis in education.

The calling of the 2017 general election illustrates the enduring power of the prime minister to override constitutional checks (such as the Fixed-term Parliaments Act) and dissolve Parliament with the permission of the monarch. However, the unexpected loss of the slender Tory majority demonstrates that the vagaries of 'events' — such as the surge in young voters backing Labour and the terror attacks during the campaign which undermined May's record as Home Secretary — can be equally potent.

The outcome of the June 2017 general election dealt Theresa May's power and prestige as prime minister a significant blow. May had called the election to 'strengthen her hand' in the forthcoming Brexit negotiations, hoping that the significant Tory poll lead would translate itself into seats, demonstrating that her policies and positions — not just in terms of leaving the EU, but in other areas such as school selection and devolution — were firmly backed by the people. Instead of reinforcing her ability to dictate events, the election result left Theresa May 'beleaguered' in the eyes of the world's press, requiring her to dismiss her closest advisers and retain ministers such as Chancellor Philip Hammond, with whom she had a difficult relationship.

Exam tip

Blair's other constitutional reforms (particularly reforming the House of Lords and enacting the Human Rights Act) provide further examples of executive policy making, as does the passing of the Constitutional Reform Act 2005.

Exam tip

When responding to the impact that prime ministers and senior colleagues can have on policy making, ensure that you are able to provide examples from before and after 1997.

Summary

After studying this topic you should be able to:
- Define key terms such as 'core executive', 'cabinet committee' and 'collective cabinet responsibility'.
- Understand the compositions and functions of the core executive, in particular how policy is made.
- Understand the relationship between the prime minister and the cabinet.

- Be clear on the differences between individual ministerial responsibility and collective cabinet responsibility, using a range of historical and contemporary examples to illustrate your understanding.
- Understand the extent to which the prime minister and the cabinet have the power to dictate events and determine policy making, using a range of examples to support evaluation and analysis.

■ The judiciary

The composition of the judiciary and the appointments process

The structure of the UK judiciary

The UK judiciary does not exist as a single body. Scotland and Northern Ireland operate under slightly different judicial arrangements than those in place in England and Wales.

The one feature common to all three systems is the part played by the UK Supreme Court, which acts as the highest court of appeal from the Court of Appeal in England and Wales, the Court of Session in Scotland and the Court of Appeal in Northern Ireland.

The structure of the judiciary in England and Wales

Figure 2 shows the structure of the judiciary in England and Wales.

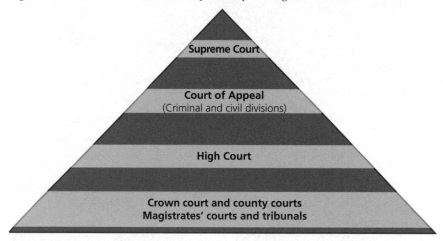

Figure 2 The hierarchy of the courts in England and Wales

What do judges do?

All judges are involved in ensuring that the law is properly applied when hearing cases under civil law and criminal law. Civil law is law that is concerned with interrelationships between different individuals and groups. Civil cases generally involve matters such as contracts or wills. Most successful cases result in compensation awards. Criminal law is law that deals with crimes by an individual or group against the state, e.g. violent behaviour, serious fraud or burglary. Such cases are normally brought by the state and can lead to fines and/or imprisonment.

■ At the lower levels of the judiciary, the main role of magistrates and judges is to preside over trials, give guidance to the jury and impose sentences. Magistrates also have the task of identifying cases that are indictable, i.e. serious enough to require a trial by jury.

Judiciary In normal usage the term refers collectively to all UK judges, from lay magistrates and those serving on tribunals right up to the 12 senior justices sitting in the UK Supreme Court.

Exam tip

It is the higher levels of the judiciary (i.e. the top two tiers of the pyramid) that are of most concern to students of Politics. These higher tiers have the power to set legal precedent, thereby establishing common law; they clarify the meaning of the law — as opposed to simply applying the letter of the law.

- At the High Court level, judges hear more serious cases and can also hear cases on appeal.
- At the Court of Appeal level and above, judges are concerned with clarifying the meaning of the law rather than just applying it; these courts can set legal precedent.

Cases heard in the Court of Appeal normally result from confusion in the lower courts regarding the meaning of a law. The Supreme Court hears cases on appeal from the Court of Appeal. In recent years such disputes have increasingly been brought under the HRA (1998) or under EU law.

Principles that underpin the work of the UK judiciary

The rule of law

The rule of law is a key doctrine of the UK Constitution under which justice is guaranteed to all. A.V. Dicey saw the rule of law as one of the 'twin pillars' of the Constitution, the other being parliamentary sovereignty.

A.V. Dicey's three strands of the rule of law

- That no one can be punished without trial.
- That no one is above the law and all are subject to the same justice.
- That the general principles of the Constitution, such as personal freedoms, result from judges' decisions rather than from parliamentary statute.

Judicial independence and judicial neutrality

The rule of law clearly demands that judges at all levels of the UK judiciary should operate with a high level of independence and dispense justice with a degree of neutrality. However, it is important to draw a clear distinction between judicial independence and judicial neutrality. The absence of judicial independence will threaten judicial neutrality — because if judges are subject to external control, their impartiality will be compromised. However, judicial independence does not guarantee judicial neutrality — because judges may still allow their personal views to influence their administering of justice.

How is the independence of the judiciary maintained?

Judicial independence in the UK is based upon five main pillars:

1 Judges are appointed for a term limited only by the requirement that they must retire by the age of 75. This means that politicians cannot seek to bring influence to bear by threatening to sack or suspend judges.
2 Judges' salaries are paid automatically from the Consolidated Fund as 'standing services'. This means that politicians are unable to manipulate judges' salaries as a way of controlling them.
3 The offence of contempt of court that exists under the so-called sub judice rules prevents the media, ministers and other individuals from speaking out publicly during legal proceedings in an attempt to influence judges or members of the jury.

Knowledge check 29

Explain what is meant by the term 'legal precedent'.

Judicial independence
The principle that those in the judiciary should be free from political control. Such independence allows judges to 'do the right thing' and apply justice properly, without fear of the consequences.

Judicial neutrality
Where judges operate impartially (i.e. without personal bias) in their administration of justice. Judicial neutrality is an essential requirement of the rule of law.

4 The creation of an independent Judicial Appointments Commission under the Constitutional Reform Act (CRA, 2005) brought greater transparency to the process of judicial appointments, thereby reducing the risk of any political bias in judicial appointments.

5 Most senior judges serve a long apprenticeship as barristers and therefore take considerable pride in their personal legal standing. They will not simply defer to politicians or public opinion if they think that doing so would compromise their judicial integrity.

How is judicial neutrality guaranteed?

It is impossible to guarantee judicial neutrality because judges will inevitably bring some degree of personal bias to their work. However, the promise of a universal application of the law under the doctrine of the rule of law requires that such bias is not allowed to colour judicial decisions.

There are four main ways in which this goal is achieved:

1 Relative anonymity: until recently, senior judges rarely spoke out publicly on issues of law or public policy, and they are still expected to avoid being drawn into open defence of their rulings, or criticism of those in government.

2 Restrictions on political activity: judges are not permitted to campaign on behalf of a political party or a pressure group. Their political views or outlook should not become a matter of public record.

3 Legal basis for all judgments: senior judges are generally expected to offer an explanation of how their decisions are rooted in law, leaving less room for personal bias.

4 High-level training: judges are part of a highly trained profession, regulated by the Law Society. Elevation to the higher ranks of the judiciary would normally reflect a belief that they are able to put aside any personal bias they might hold when administering justice.

> **Knowledge check 30**
>
> Explain the distinction between judicial independence and judicial neutrality.

The appointment of senior judges below Supreme Court level

Appointments to the **senior judiciary** were once made by the monarch on the advice of the prime minister and the Lord Chancellor, with the Lord Chancellor consulting serving senior judges through a process known as 'secret soundings'. These are the informal and secretive ways in which most senior UK judges were once appointed. The phrase describes the way in which the Lord Chancellor consulted in secret with close associates and those already serving in the senior judiciary. The resulting lack of transparency in appointments led to accusations of elitism.

It was said that this system lacked transparency, compromised the separation of powers, and resulted in a senior judiciary drawn almost exclusively from a very narrow social circle: public school and Oxbridge educated, white, male and beyond middle age. Although lower-level vacancies in the senior judiciary (e.g. for High Court judges) were advertised from the 1990s, the Lord Chancellor did not have to fill vacant posts from the ranks of those who had applied.

> **Senior judiciary**
> Comprising justices of the Supreme Court, heads of divisions, Lords Justices of Appeal, High Court judges and deputy High Court judges.

Reform of the process under New Labour

The Constitutional Reform Act (2005) reduced the power of the Lord Chancellor and placed most senior judicial appointments into the hands of a new, independent Judicial Appointments Commission (JAC). It was hoped that this change would enhance the separation of powers and result in a senior judiciary that was more socially representative of the broader population. The JAC's mission statement even includes a commitment to appoint 'on merit and merit alone [using] selection processes that are open and fair to all applicants, regardless of their gender, race or background'.

According to the Justice Department, however, even at the start of 2017:

- only 21% of High Court judges and 21% of Court of Appeal judges were women
- only 5% of High Court judges and 0% of Court of Appeal judges were from a Black, Asian or Minority Ethnic (BAME) background.

The appointment of Supreme Court justices

The founding justices of the new Supreme Court were those Law Lords in post on 1 October 2009, the start of the legal year. Although these 11 individuals remained members of the House of Lords, they were barred from sitting and voting in the upper chamber for as long as they remained justices of the new Supreme Court.

In order to be considered for appointment as a justice of the Supreme Court today, candidates must have either held high judicial office for at least 2 years or been a **qualifying practitioner** for a period of 15 years.

Vacancies in the Supreme Court are filled not by the regular JAC but by an ad hoc, five-member selection commission comprising:

- the president of the Supreme Court
- the deputy president of the Supreme Court
- one member of the JAC
- one member of the Judicial Appointments Board for Scotland
- one member of the Northern Ireland Judicial Appointments Commission.

This ad hoc commission recommends a single name to the Lord Chancellor for his or her consideration. The Lord Chancellor (the Justice Secretary) can accept the recommendation, reject the nomination, or request more information from the commission. Although the appointments procedure still involves a government minister, their input is greatly reduced as they are not permitted repeatedly to reject names put forward by the ad hoc selection commission.

Does the Supreme Court 'look like the UK'?

Although one would hardly expect a superior court such as the UK Supreme Court to be entirely socially representative of the broader population — due to the qualifications for office and the importance of the role — the membership of the Court has left it open to accusations of elitism. Such concerns have not been dispelled by appointments to the Court between 2009 and 2017.

Qualifying practitioner
Someone who has a senior courts qualification, is an advocate in Scotland or a solicitor entitled to appear in the Scottish Court of Session and the High Court of Justiciary, or is a member of the Bar of Northern Ireland or a solicitor of the Court of Judicature of Northern Ireland.

Exam tip

Before the creation of the Supreme Court, the most senior judges in the land, the Law Lords, had seats in the House of Lords. Under the terms of the Constitutional Reform Act (2005) those justices appointed to the Supreme Court are not automatically awarded peerages, thus enhancing the separation of powers.

The role of the Supreme Court and its impact on government, legislature and the policy process

Why was the UK Supreme Court established?

Before the UK Supreme Court began its work in October 2009, the highest court of appeal in the UK comprised the 12 Law Lords who sat in the Appellate Committee of the House of Lords. The UK Supreme Court was established under the terms of the 2005 Constitutional Reform Act in response to a number of longstanding concerns regarding the place of these Law Lords within our system of government.

The Supreme Court was established in place of the Law Lords due to:

- concerns over the partial 'fusion of powers' present in the UK system — specifically, the position of the Lord Chancellor in all three branches of government and the fact that the Law Lords sat in the upper chamber of the legislature, in addition to their judicial role
- a lack of transparency in the way in which Law Lords were appointed
- confusion over the work of the Law Lords — in particular, a widespread failure to understand the distinction between the House of Lords' legislative and judicial functions.

What functions does the Supreme Court perform?

Under the CRA (2005) the new UK Supreme Court took on the judicial functions previously performed by the Law Lords:

- To act as the final court of appeal in England, Wales and Northern Ireland — and hear appeals from civil cases in Scotland.
- To clarify the meaning of the law and establish legal precedent — by hearing appeals in cases where there is uncertainty over the law.

The constitutional position of the Court

Whereas the US Supreme Court can declare Acts of Congress unconstitutional, thereby striking them down, the UK Supreme Court has no such power in respect of parliamentary statute. This is because statute law remains the supreme source of constitutional law in the UK. In spite of this, the UK Supreme Court still wields considerable influence through its use of judicial review (see below).

The importance of ultra vires, judicial review and the Supreme Court's interactions with and influence over the legislative and policy-making processes

Judicial review and ultra vires

As we have seen, the Supreme Court and the Courts of Appeal that operate directly below it are of most interest to students of Politics because these higher tiers of the judiciary have the power to set legal precedent (i.e. establish **common law**) through

---

Knowledge check 31

What criticism could be made of the composition of the current UK Supreme Court? In what ways could such a socially unrepresentative composition be explained or defended?

Common law The body of legal precedent resulting from the rulings of senior judges. Sometimes referred to as case law or judge-made law, it is an important source of the UK Constitution.

their use of **judicial review**. In short, these higher courts clarify the meaning of the law — in a sense, even 'making law' — as opposed to simply applying the letter of the law.

Ultra vires cases and the Supreme Court

The doctrine of parliamentary sovereignty and the supremacy of statute law in the UK meant that judicial review once involved little more than judges deciding whether or not a public official had operated beyond the authority granted to them under the law (i.e. acted **ultra vires**) as opposed to them questioning the basis of the law itself.

The growing power of the Supreme Court

Although the ability to make ultra vires rulings is still an important weapon in the Supreme Court's armoury, the power of the UK judiciary has been enhanced by two key developments in recent years:

- the growing importance of European Union law
- the impact of the Human Rights Act (1998).

European Union law and the Supreme Court

Under the European Communities Act (1972), the UK incorporated the Treaty of Rome into UK law. The effect of this simple change was to give European laws precedence over conflicting UK statutes, whether past or present.

Supreme Court Justice Lord Mance argued that Parliament gave the European Court of Justice a blank cheque when it drafted the 1972 European Communities Act in such a way as to give EU law a higher status, saying that 'no explicit constitutional buttress remains against any incursion by EU law whatever'.

For many years this simply meant that the UK government could be called to account at the European Court of Justice. However, in the wake of the Factortame case (1990), UK courts have been able to 'suspend' UK statutes that appear to violate EU law. The case took its name from a Spanish-owned fishing company, Factortame Limited, which had challenged the legality of the Merchant Shipping Act (1988) under European law.

European Court of Justice (ECJ)

- The 'supreme court' of the European Union.
- Hears cases arising under EU law.
- Based in Luxembourg.

Judicial review The process by which judges review the actions of public officials or public bodies in order to determine whether or not they have acted in a manner that is lawful.

Ultra vires From the Latin, meaning 'beyond the authority' or 'beyond one's powers'. The process of judicial review can be used to determine whether or not a minister or other government officer has acted ultra vires — that is, beyond the authority granted to them in law.

Case study 1

The Supreme Court in Action
United States of America v *Nolan* (2015)

This case resulted from a claim against the US government under the Trade Union and Labour Relations Act 1992. Nolan, who had been employed by the US Army in a base in Hampshire, had argued that there should have been more consultation with workers' representatives before she was made redundant. The US government argued that the Secretary of State had acted ultra vires under the European Communities Act (1972) because the regulations under which Nolan had made her original claim went beyond the basic rights given under EU law.

The Supreme Court found in Nolan's favour, arguing that the Secretary of State had acted within the powers granted to him when issuing regulations in 1995.

Knowledge check 32

What does this case tell us about the nature and complexity of the Supreme Court's work?

The Supreme Court and the HRA (1998)

The European Convention on Human Rights (ECHR, 1950) was established by the Council of Europe, an intergovernmental body that is separate from the European Union and not to be confused with the EU's Council of Ministers or European Council. Alleged violations of the ECHR are investigated by the European Commission on Human Rights and tried in the European Court of Human Rights, based in Strasbourg. Again, these bodies are not to be confused with the EU's European Commission and European Court of Justice.

Although cases brought under the ECHR were once routinely heard at the European Court of Human Rights, by incorporating the ECHR into UK law, the HRA allowed citizens to pursue cases under the ECHR through UK courts from October 2000.

Knowledge check 33

Explain the differences between the European Court of Human Rights (ECtHR) and the European Court of Justice (ECJ).

European Court of Human Rights (ECtHR)

- Established by the Council of Europe.
- Hears cases brought under the European Convention on Human Rights.
- Based in Strasbourg — but it is not an EU institution.

The extent of the Supreme Court's power under the HRA

As we have seen, the HRA does not have the same legal status as EU law or the US Bill or Rights, with the latter being both entrenched and superior to regular statute. As a regular piece of statute, the HRA can be amended, 'suspended' (derogated) — in its entirety or in part — or simply repealed, like any Act.

However, while the courts cannot strike down parliamentary statute under the HRA, they can make a declaration of incompatibility, thus inviting Parliament to reconsider the offending statute. Furthermore, where statute law is silent or unclear, the courts can make even greater use of the HRA by using its provision to establish legal precedent in common law. In addition, we should remember that the HRA has a hidden influence through the process by which draft legislation is now examined by Parliament's Joint Committee on Human Rights in order to ensure that it is HRA-compatible.

Exam tip

Under the HRA, the Supreme Court is able to issue a declaration of incompatibility only where a parliamentary statute appears to violate the rights guaranteed — and Parliament is not obliged to amend the offending statute. That said, the HRA (like the ECHR) has a 'persuasive authority' that has enhanced the protection of individual rights in the UK.

Case studies 2 and 3 illustrate the extent of the ultra vires power and its limitations, while also demonstrating the extent of the judiciary's power under the European Convention on Human Rights, and the Human Rights Act that incorporates that Convention into UK law.

Case study 2

The Supreme Court in Action

Reilly v *Secretary of State for Work and Pensions* (2016)

Reilly argued that in requiring her to work for a private company in order to receive state benefits, the Department of Work and Pensions (DWP) had infringed the protection against slavery provided in Article 4 of the European Convention on Human Rights.

On appeal in 2013, the Supreme Court concluded that while the DWP's 'Welfare to Work' scheme had not established slavery, it was unlawful because the DWP had acted in a manner that was ultra vires, i.e. beyond the authority given to it by Parliament.

By the time of the ruling, the government had already passed the Jobseekers (Back to Work Schemes) Act 2013, which changed the law retrospectively so that no offence had been committed. In 2016, the Court of Appeal eventually ruled that changing the law retrospectively in this way was incompatible with Article 6 of the ECHR (which guarantees the right to a fair trial) but confirmed that it was up to the government and Parliament to decide how to proceed in light of that declaration of incompatibility.

Case study 3

The Supreme Court in Action

Tigere v *Secretary of State for Business, Innovation and Skills* (2015)

Beaurish Tigere arrived in the UK from Zambia, aged six, and had completed her A-levels in the country. She was not eligible for a student loan for her undergraduate degree because she would not be able to apply to the UK Border Agency for indefinite leave to remain in the UK until 2018. In 2015, the UK Supreme Court accepted her appeal on the grounds that the negative impact on the appellant's rights under Article 2 of the ECHR (the right to education) and also Article 14 (prohibiting discrimination) could not be justified.

Has the UK judiciary had a greater impact on the work of the executive and Parliament in recent years?

In reducing the role of Lord Chancellor and removing the UK's most senior judges from the House of Lords, the Constitutional Reform Act (2005) appeared to enhance judicial independence by making it more likely that judges would feel able to hold

Knowledge check 34

Explain how case study 2 helps us to understand the limitations on the status of the ECHR (HRA) in UK law.

Knowledge check 35

The Tigere case was decided under the ECHR provisions that are enshrined in the HRA. What options would the government have if it was not prepared to accept the Court's ruling? Explain your answer.

the executive and Parliament to account. However, the physical relocation of the UK's top court to its new accommodation in Middlesex Guildhall in 2009, though highly symbolic, did little to change the legal–constitutional relationship between the judiciary, the executive and the legislature (Parliament).

The key to explaining the growing importance of the judiciary in relation to the other two branches of government is understanding the way in which EU law and the HRA have drawn senior judges into the political arena.

The HRA, the executive and Parliament

By allowing cases under the ECHR to be heard in UK courts, the HRA (1998) allowed the UK's most senior judges to directly question Acts of Parliament, as well as the actions of those working in the executive. However, although the HRA gives judges the right to issue a 'declaration of incompatibility' where an Act of Parliament appears to have violated the ECHR, Parliament is under no legal obligation to fall into line with the Court's ruling. Moreover, even where senior judges rule that ministers acted beyond their statutory authority (i.e. ultra vires), those very ministers can use the executive's control of Parliament to pass retrospective legislation legitimising their earlier actions.

EU law, the executive and Parliament

The precedent established under the Factortame case (1990) allows senior judges to suspend the actions of both Parliament and the executive, where either branch appears to have breached EU law. Moreover, the extension of EU law in the wake of the Maastricht Treaty (1992) brought senior UK judges into conflict with both the executive and Parliament across a far wider range of policy areas than had previously been the case. Although the scope and scale of EU law have grown significantly since Maastricht, however, many areas of public policy remain largely in the hands of Parliament, thus limiting the scope of judicial action under EU law.

The overall impact of the UK Supreme Court

The UK does not have an entrenched, codified and supreme constitutional document, a set of 'fundamental laws' akin to the US Constitution. As we have seen, therefore, it is impossible for the UK Supreme Court to 'strike down' Acts of Parliament or move against the government in the style in which its US counterpart can tear up Acts of Congress and force the president to back down.

The Court's power is therefore limited to those four main areas identified over the course of this chapter.

The extent of Supreme Court power

- Revisiting and reviewing earlier legal precedent established under common law and case law ('judge-made law').
- Making ultra vires rulings where the Court judges that public bodies have acted beyond their statutory authority.
- Addressing disputes arising under EU law.
- Issuing 'declarations of incompatibility' under the Human Rights Act (1998).

Exam tip

It is important to note that the recent increase in judicial action has had a further, indirect, impact, with those in the executive and in Parliament now looking to head off potential conflict in the courts by ensuring that all legislation is HRA-compliant and EU-compliant.

Knowledge check 36

Using the information provided as well as material drawn from your own research, write two paragraphs evaluating the significance of the Human Rights Act in relation to the power of the Supreme Court:

- One paragraph should argue that the HRA has only a limited impact on the power of senior judges such as those who sit in the UK Supreme Court.
- The other paragraph should argue that the HRA has led to the UK Supreme Court developing into an institution far more powerful than the Law Lords that it replaced.

Lord Phillips' prediction that the creation of the new Supreme Court would be a change of 'form rather than of substance' has largely been borne out. The 'key cases' that Lord Neuberger, president of the Court, identified, in an article marking the first five years of the Court, clearly do not represent a significant departure from what the Law Lords might have done previously.

Key Supreme Court cases identified by Lord Neuberger

R v Horncastle & Others (2009) Unsubstantiated evidence from others that is not given under oath in court (so-called 'hearsay evidence') can be used as a basis for conviction.

Al Rawi v the Security Service (2011) Outlawed the use of secret evidence in court by the intelligence services.

Prest v Petrodel Resources Ltd (2013) Property belonging to a company (i.e. company assets) should normally be seen as separate from property belonging to individuals.

R (HS2 Action Alliance Limited) v Secretary of State for Transport (2014) EU directives did not require the government to consult more widely over the HS2 rail project.

R (Nicklinson) v Ministry of Justice (2014) Article 8 of the ECHR could not be used over the Suicide Act (1961) as a means of justifying assisted suicide.

Is the Supreme Court too powerful?

Such questions are generally rooted in the notion that there has been a blurring of the traditional distinction between those politicians who 'make' the law and the judges who should simply 'apply' it: that senior judges have become little more than 'politicians in robes'. In a sense, such a distinction will clearly always be flawed as a result of the role that senior judges play in interpreting and clarifying the law when resolving those disputes that arise under it. The Supreme Court's ability to establish precedent through common law could therefore be seen as a quasi-legislative power.

Critics also argue that the way in which senior judges have been drawn into the political fray in recent years as a result of measures such as the Human Rights Act (1998) has resulted in a further politicisation of the judiciary. Politicisation is the process by which individuals traditionally regarded as being beyond the party political fray are drawn into it. Politicisation of the judiciary is said to result from appointments being made on political grounds as opposed to being truly meritocratic. The way in which the UK judiciary was drawn into areas of political controversy in the wake of the HRA (1998) was also seen by some as evidence of politicisation.

However, while some see this growing public profile and increased conflict between senior judges and politicians as posing a threat to judicial neutrality, it could just as easily be seen as evidence of growing independence and neutrality, not least because senior judges appear increasingly willing to take on the political establishment in defence of civil liberties.

Exam tip

Remember that any move to review the status of the Human Rights Act and/or complete Brexit would massively reduce the ability of the Supreme Court to have a significant impact on the operation of the executive or Parliament in the way it has done in recent years.

Quasi-legislative Where the impact of differences in the Court's interpretations over time can appear tantamount to a legislative change, even though Parliament has made no changes to statute law.

The potential impact of Brexit on the power or authority of the UK Supreme Court

Any UK departure from the European Union would inevitably have an impact on the status, power and authority of the UK Supreme Court. It is important, however, to distinguish between those institutions and processes which are part of the EU and those which are not.

Brexit and the Court's power under the Human Rights Act

Those who argued in favour of the UK leaving the EU have often also been the fiercest critics of the ECtHR, the body established in 1959 to hear cases arising under the 1950 ECHR. That Convention, incorporated into British law under the Human Rights Act (1998), is problematic for those who see it as a threat to the independence and sovereignty of the Westminster Parliament. Irrespective of the merits or demerits of that view, however, the reality is that the ECHR was established not by the European Union but by the Council of Europe, an entirely separate organisation founded in 1949 by Britain and nine other European states.

Thus, leaving the EU would not, in itself, remove our obligations under the ECHR, any more than repealing the HRA would. The only way to remove ourselves from the jurisdiction of the ECtHR would be to withdraw from the Convention itself, an almost unthinkable act given that all European states, with the exception of Vatican City, Belarus and Kazakhstan, are current signatories.

Brexit and the Court's power under EU law

Whereas leaving the EU would have little or no direct impact on the status of the HRA, the ECHR or the ECtHR, Brexit would involve withdrawing from the Treaty of Rome, meaning that EU law would no longer take precedence over UK law and the ECJ would no longer have jurisdiction over the UK. This would impact on the work of the UK Supreme Court:

- First, because a proportion of its current case load relates to EU law.
- Second, because the removal of a court that is in theory superior to the Supreme Court in some aspects of law would enhance its status and authority.

> **Exam tip**
>
> A decision to withdraw from the ECHR as well as the EU (removing the UK from the jurisdictions of both the ECtHR and the ECJ) would obviously leave the UK Supreme Court in a greatly enhanced position.

Summary

After studying this topic you should be able to:

- Define the term 'judiciary' and demonstrate an awareness of the structure of the UK judiciary.
- Show an understanding of the term 'legal precedent' and explain why the higher levels of the judiciary are of particular interest to students of Politics.
- Explain the meaning and significance of the 'rule of law'.
- Distinguish between the terms 'judicial independence' and 'judicial neutrality'.

- Identify and explain some of the ways in which judicial independence and neutrality are encouraged.
- Demonstrate knowledge and understanding of the way in which judges at all levels are appointed.
- Explain why the UK Supreme Court was established and what powers it was given.
- Define and explain the terms 'judicial review' and 'ultra vires'.
- Evaluate the impact of the Supreme Court on the work of the UK executive and Parliament in recent years.

■ Devolution

The roles, powers and responsibilities of the devolved bodies in the UK

Context

The UK was traditionally said to be a **unitary state**. This meant that although the United Kingdom consists of four component nations — England, Scotland, Wales and Northern Ireland — ultimate political sovereignty was held at Westminster, more specifically by Parliament and, by implication, any party that could command majority support in the House of Commons.

However, the New Labour government returned to office in the 1997 general election was elected on the basis of a manifesto that promised a programme of **devolution**, a process by which power over most of the things that affected the everyday lives of citizens would be placed in the hands of new, subnational institutions that would be better suited to serving the interests of those who lived within their jurisdiction.

In 1999, power was devolved to new institutions in Scotland, Wales and Northern Ireland, following 'Yes' votes in referendums in each nation. The new system was one of asymmetric devolution. Rather than following a standardised blueprint, the devolved bodies were granted different powers and distinctive features. The first phase of devolution saw the creation of a Scottish Parliament and executive north of the border, a National Assembly for Wales and Welsh Executive in the principality, and a Northern Ireland Assembly and power-sharing executive that administer the government of the six counties. Devolution was to be a process rather than an event, with further powers devolved thereafter.

Devolved power in Scotland

Historical context: Scotland

Scotland was an independent state with its own parliament until the 1707 Acts of Union. This international treaty saw Scotland join the Union but retain its legal system, its education system and its local government structure. Contemporary Scottish identity draws upon this history of independent statehood.

The Scottish Parliament

Composition

The Scottish Parliament comprises 129 members (MSPs) elected by the additional member system. Seventy-three MSPs (57% of the total) are elected in single-member constituencies using the first-past-the-post system; the remaining 56 MSPs (43%) are 'additional members' chosen from party lists. They are elected in eight multi-member regions, each of which elects seven members using the regional list system of proportional representation. These seats are allocated to parties on a corrective 'top-up' basis so that the distribution of seats reflects more accurately the share of the

Unitary state A state in which sovereignty is located at the centre. Central government has supremacy over other tiers of government, which it can reform or abolish.

Devolution Generally seen as a process by which the Westminster Parliament delegates power to a lower tier of government. A term commonly used when referring to the creation of devolved institutions in Scotland, Wales and Northern Ireland following New Labour's victory in the 1997 general election.

Knowledge check 37

Explain the difference between a unitary state and a federal state.

vote won by the parties. Elections were initially held every four years, but this was extended to every five years after the 2011 election.

Powers

The Scotland Act 1998 gave the new Scottish Parliament **primary legislative powers** in a range of policy areas, including law and order, health, education, transport, the environment and economic development. The Act also gave the Scottish Parliament tax-varying powers: it could raise or lower the rate of income tax in Scotland by up to 3% (i.e. 3p in the pound). However, these powers have not been used.

The Scotland Act 2012 gave the parliament the power to vary income tax up or down by 10% as well as devolving further powers to Scotland — for example, the regulation of controlled drugs. The Act also allowed the Scottish government to borrow up to £2.2 billion each year.

Limits on the Scottish Parliament's legislative powers were established by the Scotland Act 1998. It specified several policy areas in which the Scottish Parliament has no legislative authority. These 'reserved powers' remain the sole responsibility of Westminster.

> **Primary legislative powers** The authority to legislate within a given jurisdiction without having to seek the approval of some higher legislative body.

Powers reserved to the Westminster Parliament

- UK constitution.
- Defence and national security.
- Foreign policy, including relations with the EU.
- Fiscal, economic and monetary systems.
- Common market for British goods and services.
- Employment legislation.
- Social security (but with some areas devolved to Scotland and Northern Ireland).
- Broadcasting.
- Nationality and immigration.

Crucially, the 1998 Act also stated that Westminster remains sovereign in all matters; it had simply chosen to exercise its sovereignty by devolving legislative responsibility to a Scottish Parliament, without diminishing its own powers. Westminster retained the right to override the Scottish Parliament in areas where legislative powers had been devolved. It could, in theory, also legislate to abolish the Scottish Parliament. However, the Scotland Act 2016 states that the Scottish Parliament and government are 'a permanent part of the United Kingdom's constitutional arrangements' and cannot be abolished unless approved by a referendum in Scotland.

The Scottish government

The Scottish government, known as the Scottish Executive before 2007, draws up policy proposals and implements legislation passed by the Parliament. The first minister, usually the leader of the largest party at Holyrood, heads the Scottish government and appoints the cabinet. At the time of writing, the SNP's Nicola Sturgeon had been first minister since 2014.

> **Knowledge check 38**
>
> Study the list of reserved powers in the box. Why are such powers reserved to the Westminster Parliament when things such as education policy and health policy are devolved to the Scottish government?

A road to Scottish independence?

The creation of the Scottish Parliament proved to be the beginning of a process of devolution rather than its end point. Pressure for further devolution grew, particularly after the SNP won power in 2007. The UK government set up the Calman Commission to consider further devolution but not independence. Its 2009 report recommended that the Scottish Parliament be given greater tax-varying powers, responsibility for some other taxes and duties, and for policy on issues such as drink-driving and speed limits. The Scotland Act 2012 duly devolved a range of powers, including the power to set a Scottish rate of income tax.

The independence referendum (2014)

Having won a majority of seats at the 2011 Scottish Parliament election, the SNP pledged to hold a referendum on independence. The constitution is a reserved power: the responsibility of Westminster rather than the Scottish Parliament. However, the UK government recognised the momentum for a referendum and in 2012 prime minister David Cameron and Scottish first minister Alex Salmond signed the Edinburgh Agreement. It gave the Scottish Parliament temporary powers to hold a referendum in 2014 and reduced the voting age from 18 to 16 for the referendum. The SNP had initially suggested that voters might choose between the status quo, further devolution and independence in the referendum. But it subsequently accepted the Electoral Commission's recommendation that the referendum ask: 'Should Scotland be an independent country?'

The referendum on 18 September 2014 saw 55.3% vote 'No' to an independent Scotland. But 1.6 million voters (44.7%) supported independence. Four local authority areas — Glasgow, Dundee, West Dunbartonshire and North Lanarkshire — saw a majority 'Yes' vote. Turnout, at 84.5%, was very high in comparison with other such ballots.

The Scotland Act (2016)

In the final stages of the referendum campaign the leaders of the three main UK parties promised to deliver further devolution in the event of Scotland voting to remain within the UK. The Conservative–Liberal Democrat coalition subsequently established the independent Smith Commission which recommended the devolution of a further raft of powers, most of which were approved in the Scotland Act (2016).

The provisions of the Scotland Act (2016)

- Devolved institutions in Scotland were essentially recognised as permanent by the requirement for there to be a referendum before either the Scottish Parliament or the Scottish government could be abolished.
- Devolved institutions were granted new powers over taxation, being allowed to set the rates and thresholds for income tax as well as gaining control of 50% of VAT levies.
- These changes meant that, for the first time, the Scottish government was responsible for raising more than 50% of the money that it spends.
- The Scottish Parliament was given legislative power over a range of new areas, including road signs, speed limits and some welfare benefits.
- The Scottish government was given control over its electoral system, although a two-thirds supermajority in the Scottish Parliament was required for any change.

The Scotland Act 2016 did not go far enough for the SNP, and it falls short of 'devo-max' in which the Scottish Parliament would have full responsibility for all taxes, duties and spending (i.e. 'full fiscal autonomy'). But the Act marks a major extension of devolution by creating Scottish tax and welfare systems that differ from those in the rest of the UK. It is also worth noting that the Scottish Parliament now has greater powers than subnational governments in many other European states.

The general election, 2017

The result of the 2017 general election dented both the Scottish National Party and the Scottish independence cause itself, although the overall results mask more complex factors at work. Ultimately the SNP lost more than a third of its Westminster seats (falling from 56 to 35), with party 'big beasts' Alex Salmond and Angus Robertson among some high-profile casualties. While party leader Nicola Sturgeon admitted that plans for a second independence referendum were 'undoubtedly' a factor as the party lost nearly half a million voters from 2015, post-election polling data revealed that former SNP voters who also voted 'Leave' in the EU referendum were the biggest group to desert the SNP over its prominent support for 'Remain'.

In contrast, the main beneficiaries of the SNP's decline were the Scottish Conservatives led by Ruth Davidson. Davidson's Conservative candidates managed to connect with Scottish voters on issues such as farming, fishing and energy in ways that the perceived independence-obsessed SNP had failed to, leading many to conclude that the issue of Scottish independence has been mothballed for some years to come.

Devolved power in Wales

Historical context: Wales

Wales entered the Union in 1536 when England completed its conquest of the principality. It was governed from London but retained a distinctive culture, in spite of Anglicisation. The 2011 census found that 19% of people in Wales were able to speak the Welsh language.

The National Assembly of Wales (Welsh Assembly)

Composition

The National Assembly for Wales, commonly known as the Welsh Assembly, has 60 members elected by the additional member system. Of these, 40 members are elected in single-member constituencies using the first-past-the-post system, and 20 in five multi-member regions using the list system. Elections were initially held every four years but this was extended to every five years by the Wales Act 2014.

Powers

The Welsh Assembly was initially weaker than the Scottish Parliament. It had secondary legislative powers and executive powers, but no primary legislative authority. This meant that it could 'fill in the details' of, and implement, legislation passed by the Westminster Parliament only in policy areas such as education and health.

Secondary legislative powers The right to administer or vary policy within a particular jurisdiction under the authority of some higher legislative body.

The Government of Wales Act 2006 enabled the Assembly to ask for further powers to be transferred from Westminster, and permitted the Assembly to gain primary legislative powers if this was approved in a referendum. With the main parties supportive, the 2011 referendum produced a 64% vote in favour. The Assembly duly gained the power to make primary legislation in 20 devolved areas. These had been specified in the Government of Wales Act 1998 and included education, health, transport, the environment and economic development.

The Wales Act (2014) was the UK government's response to the Silk Commission's recommendations on further devolution to Wales. Although it was fairly modest in scope, the Act did transfer control of some smaller taxes to devolved institutions in Wales. It also put in place a mechanism by which devolution of other lower-level taxes could be achieved, with the approval of the Westminster Parliament, and provided the legal framework required for a Welsh referendum on the partial devolution of income tax. Symbolically, the Act also changed the name of the Welsh executive from the Welsh Assembly government to the Welsh government.

The Wales Act (2017) reinforced the primary legislative authority that devolved institutions in Wales had been granted in the wake of the 2011 Welsh referendum. This Act also paved the way for the National Assembly of Wales to set Welsh rates of income tax from April 2019, without the need for the kind of referendum envisaged under the Wales Act (2014).

The Welsh government

The Welsh government, known as the Welsh Assembly government before 2011, formulates and implements policy. The first minister (originally first secretary), who is normally the leader of the largest party in the assembly, heads the Welsh government and appoints the cabinet. Labour's Carwyn Jones became first minister in 2009.

In the same way that the Scotland Act (2016) offered a degree of permanence to devolved arrangements north of the border, the Wales Act (2017) similarly required a referendum before the abolition of either the Welsh Assembly or the Welsh government.

Devolved power in Northern Ireland

> ### Historical context: Northern Ireland
>
> The island of Ireland had joined the Union in 1800 through an Act of Union. However, the Union was a troubled one, with the 'Irish Question' a long-running and difficult issue in British politics. Demands for home rule eventually led to the partition of Ireland in 1922. The six counties of Northern Ireland chose to remain part of the UK, with the rest of Ireland forming the Irish Free State, which became Eire under the terms of the 1937 Irish Constitution.

The long road to the Good Friday Agreement (1998)

The main political divide in Northern Ireland is that between **unionists** and **nationalists**. Unionists want Northern Ireland to remain part of the UK. Nationalists, often referred to as republicans, favour constitutional change, such as a united Ireland or a greater role for the Irish Republic in the affairs of Northern Ireland. Unionists

---

Knowledge check 39

Explain why a referendum might be seen as an appropriate way of approving a change such as the abolition of the Welsh government or the Welsh Assembly.

Unionist Adherent of a political position in Northern Ireland that supports the continued union between Great Britain and Northern Ireland.

Nationalist Adherent of a political position in Northern Ireland that supports constitutional means of achieving improved rights for Catholics and the eventual incorporation of the six counties of Northern Ireland into the Republic of Ireland.

identify with the British state and tend to be Protestant, whereas nationalists identify themselves as Irish and tend to be Catholic.

From 1922 to 1972, the Stormont Parliament and executive was responsible for the government of Northern Ireland. It was dominated by unionist politicians who represented the Protestant unionist majority and pursued policies that discriminated against the Catholic, largely republican, minority. The civil rights movement and the Irish Republican Army (IRA) took up Catholic grievances in the 1960s. British troops were sent to the province in 1969, but as 'the Troubles' escalated, the UK government suspended the Stormont Parliament in 1972. **Direct rule** from London was imposed: UK government ministers and Northern Ireland Office officials took policy decisions, not local politicians. Subsequent British governments introduced a series of unsuccessful initiatives to bring about **power-sharing devolution**, but the IRA's terrorist campaign continued.

However, years of negotiations between the UK and Irish governments, and some of the Northern Irish political parties, eventually resulted in the 1998 Good Friday Agreement — and with it, the creation of a number of new institutions.

The Northern Ireland Assembly

Composition

The Assembly consists of 108 members, elected by the single transferable vote system of proportional representation. The number of Assembly members is expected to be cut to 90 ahead of the 2021 elections. Elections initially took place every four years, but this was increased to five years after the 2011 elections.

Powers

The Northern Ireland Assembly was granted legislative powers over a similar range of policy areas to the Scottish Parliament. It was not given tax-raising powers, although corporation tax was devolved in 2015. The Assembly is expected to reduce corporation tax to 12.5% to match the rate in the Republic.

Special procedures were established in the Assembly to ensure cross-community support from both unionist and nationalist parties. For example, a majority of Assembly members voted in favour of same-sex marriage in 2015, but the Democratic Unionist Party (DUP) blocked the legislation using the 'petition of concern' mechanism, which had been designed to safeguard the rights of the unionist and nationalist communities.

The Northern Ireland Executive

The Executive is led by a first minister and deputy first minister. The first minister is the leader of the largest party in the Assembly and the deputy first minister is drawn from the second largest party. Ministerial posts are allocated on a proportional basis according to party strength in the Assembly. The agreement thus ensures power sharing, with both unionists and nationalists represented in government. However, after the 2016 elections, the Ulster Unionist Party (UUP) and the Social Democratic and Labour Party (SDLP) declined to nominate ministers and formed the Assembly's first Official Opposition.

Intergovernmental bodies

As well as establishing the Northern Ireland Assembly and Power Sharing Executive, the Good Friday Agreement required the UK and Irish governments to amend their

Direct rule The government of Northern Ireland from London, through special procedures at Westminster.

Power-sharing devolution Form of devolution in which special arrangements are put in place to ensure that both communities in a divided society are represented in the executive and that they assent to legislation on sensitive issues.

Knowledge check 40

Undertake some background research on the situation in Northern Ireland in the 1970s and 1980s. Explain what is meant by the phrase 'the Troubles'.

constitutions to clarify the status of Northern Ireland. For example, the Irish state removed its constitutional claim to the six counties in the north. The agreement also paved the way for a new Police Service of Northern Ireland and for the early release of those imprisoned for terrorist offences associated with the Troubles. In addition, the Agreement established a number of intergovernmental bodies.

Intergovernmental bodies established under the Good Friday Agreement

- North–South Ministerial Council: in this body, the Northern Ireland executive and Republic of Ireland government cooperate on cross-border issues.
- British–Irish Council: here the UK and Irish governments, the devolved administrations in Scotland, Wales and Northern Ireland, plus the Isle of Man and Channel Islands, exchange policy ideas.
- British–Irish Intergovernmental Conference: in this the UK and Irish governments discuss the situation in Northern Ireland.

Bridging the sectarian divide

The process encountered early problems, with the UK government suspending the devolved institutions and re-imposing direct rule on four occasions as the lack of trust between the two communities persisted. Parades by the Protestant Orange Order, paramilitary activity, policing issues and, most importantly, the decommissioning of arms all threatened to derail the peace process. The IRA, the main republican paramilitary body, did not fully decommission its arms or declare explicitly that its conflict was over until 2005. Most loyalist paramilitary groups also disarmed during this period.

In a remarkable turn of events, the unionist DUP and the republican Sinn Fein agreed to work together. DUP leader Ian Paisley, dubbed 'Dr No' for his refusal to share power with Sinn Fein, and Martin McGuinness, former IRA commander in Derry/Londonderry, became first minister and deputy first minister in 2007. Paisley retired the following year and was succeeded by Peter Robinson, with Arlene Foster then becoming first minister in 2016.

The 2017 general election threw up yet more complexity for political arrangements in Northern Ireland. Some quarters hailed the DUP as 'the real winners of the 2017 general election' (*New Statesman*, June 2017). While its electoral gains were modest (it moved from 8 seats to 10), the party's influence had far wider significance for a Conservative Party short of an overall majority. A confidence and supply deal was reached on 26 June, with the DUP confirming that it would back the Conservatives in significant Commons votes. The agreement included additional funding of £1 billion for Northern Ireland and also expressed firm commitment to the Good Friday Agreement.

Debate around devolution in England

Devolution in England

Devolution in Scotland, Wales and Northern Ireland raised the spectre of 'the English question': how should England be governed in the wake of devolution? Should there

---

Knowledge check 41

This passage mentions the UK government having to suspend power sharing in Northern Ireland from time to time and re-impose direct rule. Undertake some research and write a brief paragraph setting out the kinds of circumstances in which the UK government has imposed direct rule on Northern Ireland since 1999.

be an English Parliament or some move to limit the right of those Westminster MPs representing constituencies in Scotland, Wales or Northern Ireland from voting on measures that have little or no impact on their own constituents — a form of 'English votes for English laws'?

Addressing the West Lothian question

MPs at Westminster no longer make law on matters that have been devolved to the Scottish Parliament, Welsh Assembly and Northern Ireland Assembly. This raises questions about the roles of MPs from the different parts of the UK and how much influence they should have over matters that do not directly affect their own constituents — a problem encapsulated in the so-called **West Lothian question**.

There have been a handful of cases since devolution in which legislation on 'English' issues would not have been approved without the support of MPs representing Scottish constituencies — for example, the legislation on foundation hospitals and university tuition fees in England in 2003–04. The Blair government responded to the West Lothian question by reducing the number of Scottish MPs from 72 to 59 in 2005, but this did little to satisfy those concerned at apparent inequalities in representation.

One solution to the problem would have been to establish an English Parliament, given that England is the only part of the UK not to have its own devolved legislature. An English Parliament could be granted powers over English issues on a par with those granted to the Scottish Parliament — and it needn't sit at Westminster or in London even. There is, however, little public support for an English Parliament.

English votes for English laws

A solution that gained greater traction, not least with many Conservative MPs, was the suggestion that there should be a system of **English votes for English laws**, where only those MPs representing English constituencies would be permitted to vote on measures identified as affecting England alone.

The 2013 report of the 'Commission on the consequences of devolution for the House of Commons' (also known as the McKay Commission) recommended that only English MPs should be allowed to vote on measures which were identified as affecting only England. Changes to House of Commons standing orders made in October 2015 mean that this form of 'English votes for English laws' is now in place. This new system was used for the first time in January 2016, when only those MPs representing English constituencies were permitted to vote on some elements of a Housing and Planning Bill.

Opponents of 'English votes for English laws' claim that there may be problems in determining where decisions on public spending in England affect funding in the rest of the UK. They also argue that it creates different classes of MPs and could make it difficult for a UK government to deliver on its manifesto commitments. Interestingly, only 6 of 19 UK governments elected since 1945 have had enough MPs from England alone to give them an overall majority in the House of Commons.

West Lothian question
Originally posed by Labour MP Tam Dalyell in a Commons debate in 1977, the West Lothian question asks: Why should Scottish MPs be able to vote on English matters at Westminster when English MPs cannot vote on matters devolved to the Scottish Parliament?

English votes for English laws Special procedures in the House of Commons for dealing with legislation that only affects England.

Existing devolution in England

Regional government in England

Governing London

The **Greater London Authority** (GLA) is the tier of regional government established in the capital under the Greater London Authority Act (1999) and first elected in May 2000. It has strategic responsibility for economic development, transport, planning and policing. The GLA consists of a directly elected mayor and a 25-member London Assembly. The mayor sets the budget and determines policy. The most visible mayoral initiative was the congestion charge, introduced in 2003.

The GLA is often seen as part of New Labour's devolution programme, though it was not devolution in the strictest sense of the word because the powers granted to the Authority were not previously exercised by central government.

Greater London Assembly

- A 25-member assembly created as part of the Greater London Authority.
- The Assembly scrutinises the work of the London mayor, including oversight of the mayor's budget. It can conduct investigations into matters concerning Londoners and publish reports.
- Elections to the Assembly are conducted under the additional member system.

English regional assemblies

The Blair governments also planned to create directly elected regional assemblies, with limited executive functions, in the eight English regions outside London. However, these plans were dropped when a referendum on an assembly for northeast England produced a clear 'No' vote in 2004.

Proposals for regional assemblies failed for a number of reasons:

- Few areas of England have a strong sense of regional identity.
- There is no real tradition of regional government in England.
- There was public concern about the costs of creating another layer of government and about the role of the assemblies.

Although unelected regional development agencies were created in 1999, to promote economic development, they were abolished by the Conservative–Liberal Democrat coalition in 2012.

Combined authorities

The combined authorities (see Table 7) consist of several adjoining local authorities in the English regions to which strategic functions in areas such as economic development, transport, health, planning and policing are devolved by central government. Like the mayor of London, this is an example of executive devolution in which some executive functions (e.g. control of funding and limited rights of policy

---

Knowledge check 42

Do some research on the Cornish nationalist party Mebyon Kernow ('Sons of Cornwall').

- What is it campaigning for?
- What arguments does it offer in support of its demands?

initiative) are devolved by the centre but the new bodies do not have independent law-making powers. The Greater Manchester combined authority was created in 2011; there were a total of nine such authorities by 2017.

Table 7 Combined authorities in 2017

Authority	Established
Greater Manchester	2011
Liverpool City Region	2014
North East	2014
Sheffield City Region	2014
West Yorkshire	2014
Tees Valley	2016
West Midlands	2016
Cambridgeshire and Peterborough	2017
West of England	2017

In 2017 there were 23 directly elected mayors in the UK, including several that cover more than one local authority. In May 2017, elections took place in six of these combined authority areas to elect new 'metro-mayors'. With four of the mayors representing the Conservative Party, the party declared the start of 'a new urban, Conservative agenda'.

Impact of devolution on government of the UK

Quasi-federalism

Devolution has created a new relationship between the nations that constitute the UK. Professor Vernon Bogdanor characterises the UK as a 'quasi-federal' state, a state that has some apparently federal characteristics yet retains the essential features of a unitary state.

Parliamentary sovereignty

In practice at least, parliamentary sovereignty is limited by the structures put in place under devolution. Although in purely legal terms (i.e. de jure) Westminster remains sovereign, the reality is that Scotland, Wales and Northern Ireland have essentially been granted de facto day-to-day operational independence. Moreover, as we have seen, the Scotland Act (2016) and the Wales Act (2017) require a referendum before devolved institutions in those two countries can be abolished.

Policy divergence

One obvious consequence of devolution has been the fact that social policy in the home nations is now a good deal less homogeneous than it once was. Although this phenomenon has been particularly apparent in the fields of education policy and healthcare (see Table 8), there has also been divergence in other policy areas. For example, Northern Ireland has yet to legalise same-sex marriage.

Knowledge check 43

Explain one argument in favour of the kinds of combined authorities established in the areas listed in Table 7.

Exam tip

As well as using the phrase 'quasi-federalism' as a way of explaining our constitutional arrangements post-devolution, Vernon Bogdanor has described the UK as a 'nation of nations'.

Knowledge check 44

Research examples of policy divergence across the home nations on areas of policy other than healthcare and education.

Table 8 Four examples of policy divergence in health and education post-devolution

England	Scotland	Wales	Northern Ireland
Prescription charges	Abolished	Abolished	Abolished
NHS internal market	Abolished	Abolished	Abolished
School league tables	Abolished	Abolished	Abolished
University tuition fees	No tuition fees for Scottish students at Scottish universities	Tuition fees grant for students from Wales	Lower tuition fees for Northern Irish universities

Funding the Union

The devolved administrations are funded by block grants from the UK Treasury, the size of which is settled by the Barnett formula. In 2016, the block grant for Scotland was £28 million, for Wales £14 million and for Northern Ireland £10 million. Agreed in 1978, the Barnett formula translates changes in public spending in England into equivalent changes in the block grants for Scotland, Wales and Northern Ireland, calculated on the basis of relative population. Scotland, Wales and Northern Ireland receive more public spending per head of population than England. Critics claim that this amounts to an English subsidy of the rest of the UK. However, the Barnett formula does not take account of relative needs, e.g. the health, living standards and age of the population in each nation. The transfer of powers over income tax to the Scottish Parliament under the Scotland Act (2016) will bring about a reduction in the size of its block grant from the UK government.

Summary

After studying this topic you should be able to:
- Define the term 'devolution' and demonstrate an awareness of the recent origins of devolved power within the UK.
- Distinguish between the terms 'unitary state' and 'federal state'.
- Demonstrate knowledge and understanding of the composition and roles of the main devolved institutions in Scotland, Wales and Northern Ireland.
- Show an understanding of the term 'asymmetrical devolution' as it relates to the process of devolution started by the Labour Party in the wake of the 1997 general election.
- Explain what is meant by the West Lothian question and identify the ways in which those at Westminster have sought to address it.
- Assess the extent to which political power has been devolved within England.
- Offer some evaluation of the impact of devolution on the government of the UK.

Questions & Answers

Introduction

As with any other study aid, this book is aimed at helping you develop your work (rather than helping you avoid it). It is far better to attempt the questions provided here without first reading the student answers given. Once you have done this you can review your work in light of the comments provided. You should also make a plan of how you would answer the whole question, taking account of the tips (indicated by the icon ⓔ) immediately below the question.

After each specimen question there is an exemplar answer. The commentary (indicated by the icon ⓔ that follows it) points out the answer's strengths and weaknesses. You should compare the sample answer with your own notes and amend your own notes if necessary. Having done all this, you can then attempt a full answer to the question, aiming to avoid the weaknesses but including the strengths that have been indicated in the specimen answer and explanation of the marks.

Remember that these student answers are *not* model answers for you to learn and reproduce word for word in the examination. It is unlikely that the questions in the examination will be worded exactly as they are here, and in any case, there is always more than one way of answering any question. Remember, too, that this section, which corresponds to the previous chapters, covers questions that relate to the *Government of the UK* section of the specification. Other topics and sample answers are covered in the *Politics of the UK* guide.

Assessment objectives

The assessment objectives applied at AS and A-level are:

AO1: Demonstrate knowledge and understanding of political institutions, processes, concepts, theories and issues.

AO2: Analyse aspects of politics and political information, including in relation to parallels, connections, similarities and differences.

AO3: Evaluate aspects of politics and political information, including to construct arguments, make substantiated judgements and draw conclusions.

The AS examination (one paper)

Title: *Government and Politics of the UK*

Duration: 3 hours

Total marks available: 98

Weighting: 100% of the AS

Aim to spend approximately:

- 11 minutes on each 6-mark question
- 25 minutes on each 12-mark extract-based question
- 40 minutes on each 25-mark essay question.

The A-level examination (Paper 1)

Title: *Government and Politics of the UK*

Duration: 2 hours

Total marks available: 77

Weighting: 33⅓% of the A-level

Aim to spend approximately:

- 14 minutes on each 9-mark question
- 40 minutes on the 25-mark extract-based essay question
- 40 minutes on the 25-mark essay question.

■6-mark questions (AS only)

There are four of these questions on the AS paper which are assessed using AO1 only.

What do you need to do?

■ Provide a clear and accurate definition of the concept, term or phrase identified in the question.

■ Develop your explanation and demonstrate your deeper understanding by selecting and using appropriate examples in support of your answer.

The nature and sources of the British Constitution

> Explain, with examples, the concept of an uncodified constitution.

e You should ensure that you have provided a clear and accurate definition of the term 'uncodified constitution' along with supporting examples that demonstrate what this means in practice. High-level responses will also demonstrate conceptual understanding of the difference between a constitution being 'uncodified' as opposed to 'unwritten' and contrast uncodified constitutions with the codified constitutions present in some states (e.g. the USA).

Student answer

A constitution is a set of fundamental rules (or 'fundamental law') that establishes the relationship between the state and the people, and also between those institutions that make up the state. An uncodified constitution differs from a codified constitution in that the key rules are brought together into a single, authoritative document. **a** Codified constitutions normally result from some fundamental watershed in the history of a nation (e.g. new-found independence, war and occupation, or revolution) where people have sat down with a blank sheet of paper and tried to create a new model of government. This is true of countries such as the USA, Germany and France. **b** The UK in contrast has an uncodified constitution that has evolved over time. It cannot be found in a single document but in a range of sources. It is wrong to see uncodified as meaning unwritten because some of these sources, like statute law, are written. Others, like conventions, are not. Uncodified constitutions tend to be easier to change whereas codified constitutions are often entrenched with complex amendment processes. **c**

e Level 3 (6/6 marks awarded). **a** This answer provides a clear definition. **b** Although there is probably a little too much emphasis on codified constitutions, **c** the material provides a sound foundation for the explanation of the term in question, which follows.

The structure and role of Parliament

Explain, with examples, Parliament's representative function.

ⓔ You should ensure that you have provided a clear and accurate definition of Parliament's representative function along with supporting examples of how this function is carried out. High-level responses will also demonstrate conceptual understanding of theories of representation (such as resemblance) and models of representation for individual MPs (e.g. trustee and delegate).

Student answer

MPs in the House of Commons are elected to serve a geographical constituency and all those who live there. MPs should represent the concerns of their constituents within Parliament, ⓐ ensuring that they accurately raise issues of importance not merely as delegates (mandated to represent and not deviate from a proscribed view) but as trustees, able to follow their own conscience according to the Burkean view of representation. ⓑ In practical terms, MPs also represent the interests of their political parties and the nation as a whole. Members of the Lords are not elected but still represent the national interests, and those of groups and organisations that concern them. The Lords have a particular interest in supporting the civil liberties, reflected in their resistance to the government's 'Brexit' Bill (March 2017) which they felt did not protect EU citizens effectively. ⓒ

ⓔ **Level 3 (6/6 marks awarded).** ⓐ This answer provides a clear definition, ⓑ is full of accurate knowledge of concepts and institutions, ⓒ and makes good use of relevant supporting examples.

■ 9-mark questions (A-level only)

There are three of these questions on A-level Paper 1, which are assessed using AO1 (6 marks) and AO2 (3 marks).

What do you need to do?

- Offer detailed knowledge, explanation and analysis of three distinct things as identified in the question.
- Support your answer with appropriate examples drawn from your own knowledge.
- Demonstrate a sound knowledge and understanding of relevant concepts, institutions and processes.
- Use political vocabulary accurately and appropriately.

The prime minister and cabinet

> Explain and analyse three arguments in support of the view that the cabinet remains an effective decision-making body.

ⓔ Level 3 responses will demonstrate detailed knowledge of relevant political concepts related to the cabinet's roles and functions, showing wider conceptual understanding of the decision-making processes within the executive. The highest responses will analyse three clear points within a coherent, well-exemplified answer.

Student answer

Under the coalition government (2010–15) the cabinet was a vital instrument in reaching agreements where there were conflicts between the coalition partners. Cabinet made declarations of 'agreed' policy that the rest of the coalition was expected to support. ⓐ Under these circumstances, the cabinet provided a tangible sense of coherence and unity in an otherwise unusual situation.

In addition to this, there have been a number of important decisions affecting the national interest that have led to the prime minister being either unable or unwilling to make a decision. Recent examples that involved cabinet decision making are the decision to go ahead with HS2 (high-speed rail services from London to Birmingham and beyond), the decision to hold a referendum on the possible introduction of the alternative vote for general elections, and the decision in 2010 to invest in increased nuclear energy production in the UK. ⓑ

The cabinet is still needed to manage the business of government, not least in Parliament, and to coordinate the presentation of government policy. Moreover, the cabinet is still vital in making government policies official. Cabinet decisions represent the collective will of the government and this makes them legitimate and means they will normally be supported by ministers and the rest of the governing party. ⓒ Indeed, the most recent examples of effective cabinet decision making — and support for the view that Theresa May 'restored' collegial decision making through the cabinet — can be seen in the decision to pause the go-ahead for the Hinkley Point nuclear power station and the decision over the expansion of Heathrow. ⓓ

ⓔ Level 3 (8/9 marks awarded). It may well be tempting to introduce counterarguments, but the question clearly requires three arguments *in support* of the view that the cabinet remains an effective decision-making body. **ⓐ** The first paragraph addresses the question well, with a well-structured and supported point. **ⓑ** The student follows with some effective examples in support of a second point, **ⓒ** and some sound theoretical and conceptual knowledge **ⓓ** and excellent contemporary examples.

The judiciary

> **Explain and analyse three ways in which senior judges can hold the government to account.**

ⓔ Level 3 responses will demonstrate detailed knowledge of relevant political concepts related to the roles and powers of the senior judiciary, as well as an appreciation of the way in which the judiciary can be said to have a political as well as a judicial impact. There will be a sound theoretical understanding of judicial power. Such responses will analyse three clear points within a coherent, well-exemplified answer.

Student answer

The main power at the disposal of senior judges in holding the government to account is the power of judicial review. This is where the court reviews the actions of government officials or bodies with a view to determining whether or not they have acted in line with the relevant laws or regulations. **ⓐ** Although the absence of a superior, codified and entrenched constitution means that UK judges cannot declare government actions unconstitutional, **ⓑ** there are three distinct ways in which senior judges can hold the government to account.

Firstly, **ⓒ** senior judges have always been able to use their power of judicial review to make ultra vires rulings, i.e. decide that a government minister or institution has acted beyond their/its statutory authority. Although Parliament can legislate retrospectively to 'overturn' such rulings, it is still a powerful tool in the judiciary's armoury. Michael Howard, when home secretary, was found to have acted ultra vires when he sacked the then head of the Prison Service, Derek Lewis. **ⓓ**

Secondly, **ⓒ** under the 1998 Human Rights Act (HRA), judges are able to issue a declaration of incompatibility where a piece of legislation appears to contradict the right guaranteed therein. This power was used against the use of indefinite detention of foreign terrorist suspects in the wake of 9/11. **ⓓ** The existence of such a power also has an indirect impact in that those drafting legislation take care to ensure that bills are fully HRA-compliant.

Thirdly, **c** since the Factortame case (1991), **d** judges have had the power to suspend any UK statute that appears to violate EU law, until such time as the European Court of Justice is able to make a final ruling. Although this does not amount to the power to strike down parliamentary statute, in the way in which the US Supreme Court can strike down acts of Congress, it is a significant power nonetheless.

e Level 3 (8/9 marks awarded). **a** The introduction to this response sets the scene very well indeed, **b** while also making an important point about the limitations on the power of the UK judiciary in the absence of a codified constitution. **c** The student identifies three distinct ways in which senior judges can hold the government to account. **d** They make good use of examples in support of each of the areas they analyse.

■ 12-mark extract-based questions (AS only)

There are two 12-mark questions on the AS paper, which are assessed using AO1 (2 marks), AO2 (6 marks) and AO3 (4 marks).

What do you need to do?

- Offer developed analysis and evaluation of the two extracts provided, in relation to the question posed.
- Demonstrate an understanding of different perspectives, within an analytical structure.
- Demonstrate sound knowledge and understanding of relevant concepts, institutions and processes.

Devolution

Read the extracts below and answer the question that follows.

Extract 1

From the very start of the devolution process, the Scottish Parliament was given primary legislative and tax-varying powers. The Parliament, together with the Scottish Executive, has sole responsibility for policy on issues such as education, health and local government. Some argue that the transfer of such significant powers away from Westminster means that the UK is moving away from a unitary system, with writers such as Vernon Bogdanor even using the phrase 'quasi-federalism'. Others maintain that although power has been delegated to devolved institutions, the Westminster Parliament remains sovereign.

This extract is from a weekly political journal on UK government and politics, published in 2017.

Extract 2

Although the Supreme Court accepted that Brexit will affect areas of policy that have been devolved fully to Scotland, Wales and Northern Ireland, it ruled that the UK government was under no legal obligation to consult or seek the consent of the devolved legislatures before triggering Article 50 and embarking upon the process of taking the UK out of the European Union. This is because foreign policy (including relations with the EU) is one of those areas that was reserved to the Westminster Parliament under the terms of the devolution settlement.

This 2017 extract is based on the UCL Constitution Unit's electronic newsletter, *Monitor*, which is published three times a year. The Constitution is an independent body that conducts research into constitutional reform and the impact of political change.

Analyse, evaluate and compare the arguments presented in both of the above extracts in order to reach a conclusion on the extent to which the UK could be said to have moved towards a federal system.

(e) Higher-level responses to this question will identify and evaluate the different perspectives offered in the extracts while answering the central question of whether the UK has moved towards a federal system. They will demonstrate accurate knowledge and understanding of both the mechanics of devolution and the philosophical discussions surrounding the development of devolved institutions since 1997.

Student answer

The two extracts provided offer a slightly different view on precisely where power rests in the wake of devolution. In Extract 1, the author notes that the Scottish Parliament was given 'primary legislative powers' from the time of its creation. **a** This meant that the devolved institutions north of the border were able to make laws across a wide range of policy areas without having to seek the approval of the Westminster Parliament. **d** While devolution has followed a slightly different path in Wales and Northern Ireland, it is probably true to say that, by 2017, the devolved institutions in all three territories were able to act with a high degree of autonomy. Writers such as Bogdanor have referred to the emergence of quasi-federalism in the UK because to all intents and purposes our constitutional arrangements appear, on the surface at least, to resemble those in place in countries such as the USA — with some areas of policy in the home nations having developed along divergent paths, e.g. tuition fees and prescription charge. **a**, **d** Moreover, recent changes (e.g. the Scotland Act 2016) mean that these devolved institutions cannot be dissolved without a referendum in the country in question.

However, although the UK may appear to have moved closer to a federal model in recent years, significant powers were reserved to the Westminster Parliament at the time of devolution — and remain so to this day. For example, Westminster retains control over foreign policy (as mentioned in Extract 2). **b** This control, which includes the UK's relationship with the EU, means that the SNP-controlled government in Scotland has been unable to have a significant influence on the course of the Brexit process. **d** Moreover, there is no process by which Scotland could remain part of the EU while remaining part of the UK — and the Scottish government does not have the power to call another independence referendum, as this is another power reserved to Westminster. **c** Finally, although recent legislation means that the devolved institutions cannot be abolished without a referendum, **d** the Westminster Parliament still has the right to vary the powers devolved by means of a simple Act of Parliament. **c**

(e) **Level 4 (12/12 marks awarded).** **a** This response makes good use of the extracts. **b** There is a clear sense of how the extracts differ in perspective, as well as an attempt to put the points raised in each of the extracts into their proper context. **c** The response demonstrates a secure understanding of the legal status of devolved powers **d** and makes good use of knowledge and examples to illustrate and explain those points made in the extracts.

The prime minister and cabinet

Read the extracts below and answer the question that follows.

Extract 1

While the power of the cabinet itself is widely acknowledged to be an inconsequential check on prime ministerial decision making, the presence of the party's 'big beasts' within it — such as the particularly experienced Ken Clarke in the coalition cabinet — is an altogether different matter. Damaging resignations from mismanaged relationships have checked all prime ministers (Geoffrey Howe under Thatcher), disunity (such as Major's cabinet 'bastards') can fatally undermine even the strongest seeming premier, and constant power-brokering can prove to be particularly awkward.

This extract is adapted from Nick Gallop's AQA Government & Politics article in *Politics Review*, November 2014.

Extract 2

The traditional constitutional view is that executive power is vested in the cabinet, whose members exercise collective responsibility. But the importance of the cabinet waned in the modern era. It now plays only a limited role in decision making as many key policy decisions are taken elsewhere in the executive. Suggestions that the cabinet has joined the ranks of Walter Bagehot's 'dignified institutions' — those with a symbolic role but no real influence — are premature. As Margaret Thatcher's resignation illustrated, a prime minister who fails to recognise his or her dependence on senior cabinet colleagues risks losing office.

This extract is from a daily newspaper commenting on UK government and politics, published in 2017.

Analyse, evaluate and compare the arguments presented in both of the above extracts in order to reach a conclusion on the extent to which the cabinet provides the most effective check on prime ministerial power.

ⓔ Higher-level responses will draw out key points from the extracts, analysing the checks on prime ministerial power within wider conceptual arguments about the role of the cabinet. The highest-level responses will identify some key differences within the extracts about the nature of the relationship between the prime minister and the government.

Student answer

Both the extracts provide evidence of the power relationships between the prime minister and the cabinet. The first extract is more emphatic on the checking or constraining power of the cabinet, referring to the negative impact of 'damaging resignations' on a prime minister's power. While the second extract does point to some evidence of the cabinet as a checking influence — citing the ousting of Margaret Thatcher — the narrative leans a little more towards the cabinet as one of the 'dignified institutions' of the British Constitution. **a**

The first extract draws out points such as 'mismanaged relationships' as being a check on prime ministerial power and this is true of Blair and Brown as much as the example of Major used in the extract. After all, the cabinet, as happened ultimately to Margaret Thatcher, largely over the introduction of the poll tax in the late 1980s, can overrule a prime minister. The second extract asserts that the ultimate check on a prime minister is the cabinet, but clearly infers that on a day-to-day basis the threat is negligible. **b**

It is not just the cabinet that provides the check though. The prime minister is at the mercy of world events which may turn against him or her. This happened to both Blair and Brown. Some are the architect of events that bring about their downfall, such as Cameron in 2016. Additionally, the prime minister has to maintain the support of Parliament. Cameron, for example, was not supported by Parliament in his proposal to join the USA in taking military action in Syria.

The prime minister may also lose the support of his or her party. Arguably this is what happened to Blair when he was forced out of power in 2007. **c**

Ultimately, the support or the absence of support from influential and senior cabinet colleagues can be a genuinely constraining influence. Thatcher was forced out by her party when she failed to win enough support to continue to a second ballot of MPs in her leadership challenge. Major was required to submit to backbench MPs (particularly over Europe) on a number of occasions. Blair's control of his party declined following the Iraq War in 2003 and he faced the largest backbench rebellion of any government in the last century in the post-2005 period.

e Level 4 (10/12 marks awarded). **a** This response makes good use of the extracts, briefly citing words from both of them. **b** The student makes a good attempt at differentiating the main themes of the two extracts. **c** They also demonstrate a strong base of own knowledge about the checks on prime ministerial power that places the cabinet within context. There are a number of good examples, though the student might have drawn on the last years of the coalition government to illustrate points made.

■ 25-mark extract-based essay questions (A-level only)

There is one 25-mark question on A-level Paper 1, which is assessed using AO1 (5 marks), AO2 (10 marks) and AO3 (10 marks).

What do you need to do?

■ Demonstrate a developed knowledge and understanding of relevant institutions, processes and concepts.

■ Ensure that your response is clearly organised and analytical in style.

■ Offer a balanced and developed analysis of the extract in which the arguments presented in the extract are properly compared.

■ Evaluate the arguments presented using appropriately selected examples and arrive at a well-substantiated conclusion to the question.

The nature and sources of the British Constitution

Read the extract below and answer the question that follows.

Extract

When future historians look back, they will consider the period since Labour's election in 1997 as one of enormous and generally positive constitutional reform. Probably the most dramatic change is in Scotland, where there is now a devolved parliament with full legislative powers and an executive accountable to that parliament, now from a different political party than that of the UK government. Though there have been many doubters along the road to this constitutional success, sometimes including myself, I think that any fair-minded observer would have to conclude that, despite the tensions, devolution has been wholly positive and has improved the quality of political life both in Scotland and in the wider United Kingdom.

The United Kingdom Parliament has changed as well, with the removal of most of the hereditary peers and a consequent shift in the balance of power between Lords and Commons. At the same time the constitutional relationships between others of our great institutions have shifted as the Human Rights Act continues to change the balance of influence between the executive and the judiciary, and the Freedom of Information Act modifies that between the executive and the media.

So the last decade will certainly be marked down as a period of historic constitutional transformation. The question which faces the country after this momentous decade is what, if anything, to do next.

Source: Charles Clarke MP (2009), 'Continuing the journey towards a modern constitution for Britain', published by Unlock Democracy, a grassroots campaign for democratic reform and participation.

> Analyse, evaluate and compare the arguments in the above article over the significance of those constitutional changes that took place under New Labour between 1997 and 2010.

(e) Higher-level responses to this question require a well-developed analysis and evaluation of the arguments presented in the extract. Such analysis will inevitably be rooted in accurate knowledge and understanding of the scope and nature of the programme of constitutional reform that New Labour enacted over the course of its three terms in office.

Student answer

New Labour's three terms in office (1997–2010) saw the launch of a programme of constitutional reform that was unprecedented, both in scope and in scale. However, the precise significance of the changes enacted in this period has been the subject of considerable debate among commentators. Some, including the author of the extract, regard the period as one of 'historic constitutional transformation'. **a** Others regard it as period of unfilled promise; a time when many initiatives were launched, but few were taken through to completion.

Clarke's view that we should see devolution in Scotland as being the most dramatic change undertaken in the period clearly has some merit. The Scottish Parliament, unlike the Welsh Assembly, was given primary legislative powers from the outset, meaning that it took total control of policy north of the border in areas such as education and health. **b** Moreover, changes in the wake of that initial grant of power, and further changes completed since Clarke wrote this piece, mean that commentators such as Vernon Bogdanor now see the UK not as a unitary state but as a quasi-federal state. **c** Another way in which devolution may be seen as significant is, as Clarke recognises, by the 'tensions' it created **a** — not least, the calls for independence which ultimately led to the 2014 referendum and the debates over the West Lothian question which led to the introduction of a form of English votes for English laws. **b** One might therefore argue that Clarke's view that devolution 'has improved the quality of political life both in Scotland and in the wider United Kingdom' is open to question. **a**

A similar criticism could be levelled at Clarke's assessment of the significance of Lords reform. While removing the right of all but 92 hereditary peers to sit and vote in the chamber was clearly an historically significant step, the failure to complete the second stage of Lords reform in the wake of that first tentative step makes it significant in another way: as a 'missed opportunity'. While it is true that reform has had some impact on the relationship between the Commons and the Lords, there has been no fundamental shift in that relationship, with the Commons continuing to be the dominant chamber in our system of asymmetrical bicameralism.

In some ways, it is the passage of the Freedom of Information Act (2000) and the Human Rights Act (1998) that has had the most significance of all of the changes enacted in this period. These Acts, allied to the Constitutional Reform Act (2005), allowed for the emergence of a new 'rights culture' in the UK, one that is overseen by a reformed judiciary headed by a new UK Supreme Court. **b** Although this new court simply took on the powers previously exercised by the Law Lords, its creation was significant because it marked a growing separation of powers within the UK system, both with the changes in the role of the Lord Chancellor and the physical relocation of the UK's most senior judges from the legislature to their new premises across the road in Middlesex Guildhall. **b**

While Clarke makes mention of many of the key constitutional reforms that were implemented in the period 1997–2010, his assessment of their significance is, perhaps, overly positive. Indeed, his closing remark, that the country needs to decide 'what, if anything, to do next', ignores the fact that so many of New Labour's initiatives remained unfinished after 13 years in office. **d**

e Level 5 (22/25 marks awarded). **a** This answer is very effective in the way in which it analyses and evaluates the arguments presented in the extract. **b** The student introduces lots of good evidence as part of this evaluative process. **c** They also attempt to introduce the ideas of other writers as a means of developing analysis and offering some sense of the scope of debate between commentators. **d** The response ends with a substantiated conclusion which follows on naturally from the discussion that precedes it.

The structure and role of Parliament

Read the extract below and answer the question that follows.

Extract

In the 2015–16 session, there were 22 public bill committees. Membership, which ranges from 16 to 50, reflects party strength in the Commons and whips instruct MPs how to vote. Public bill committees may take evidence from outside experts. Finance bills and bills of constitutional significance (e.g. on the EU referendum) are scrutinised on the floor of the Commons, in a Committee of the Whole House.

Select committees have extended and enhanced parliamentary scrutiny of the executive. The overall aim of select committees is to hold government accountable for policy and decision making, and support Parliament in scrutinising legislation and government spending. They highlight important issues, bring expert contributions to debates, hold the government accountable for policy problems and issue evidence-based recommendations.

This extract is from a monthly political periodical commenting on UK government and politics, published in 2017.

Analyse, evaluate and compare the arguments in the above article over the significance of the role played by committees in the parliamentary process.

(e) Higher-level responses to this question require accurate knowledge and understanding of Parliament's legislative function and the role that public bill committees play in scrutinising government legislation and that select committees play in scrutinising government policies and the activities of many influential public and private bodies. The best responses will further develop the nature of public bill committees and select committees, reflecting upon their make-up, the limits on their power and recent reforms, together with effective examples and synoptic links.

Student answer

Parliamentary committees play a crucial role in the passage of legislation — both types of committees are active and major elements within the system of checks and balances. During the committee stage of the passage of legislation through Parliament, bills are sent to a public bill committee — known as a standing committee until 2006 — where detailed scrutiny of each clause occurs and amendments can be made. Amendments are often tabled by the government as it seeks to clarify or improve the bill. A new public bill committee is established for each bill, and is named after it. Once the bill has completed this stage, that committee is dissolved.

The role of public bill committees is to scrutinise bills following their second reading in the House of Commons — they are created (and then disbanded) to look specifically at a single bill. Select committees on the other hand are permanent and scrutinise the work and activities of government departments (such as the Home Affairs Select Committee) or across areas of government and public policy or activity (such as the Public Accounts Committee). a The work of both types of committees can be powerful and far ranging. As the extract asserts, the overall aim of committees is to hold government accountable. In this respect, while public bill committees may not play a role in discussing the principles of the bill in question, they can recommend significant changes, particularly if the law has been hurriedly or badly drafted. Similarly, select committees' power to expose, embarrass or recommend can very potent indeed. b

Legislative committees of both houses are vital in scrutinising proposed legislation. They can suggest amendments to improve legislation and the Lords committees are especially important because they contain many experts and representatives of minorities who are independent of parties. However, although public bill committees play an important role, they are relatively insignificant when compared to their US counterparts. Whereas public bill committees in the UK are ad hoc and temporary, in many modern democracies similar such committees are permanent and the legislative expertise accrued within them is substantial indeed.

In the USA, committee membership can last for decades, with members becoming hugely influential in the passage of legislation in their areas of expertise. c UK public bill committees are also short on resources, unable to force witnesses to testify before them, limited in their potency by being made up in accordance with the party composition of the Commons and with the very real prospect of all noteworthy amendments being rejected, unless government-backed, when the bill returns to the Commons. These problems are compounded by factors included in the extract and which refer to the fact that these committees reflect party strength in the Commons and whips instruct MPs how to vote. d

There are some major strengths to select committees on the other hand. They usually act in a very independent way and often reach highly critical conclusions. Many commentators concur that select committees have become, arguably, the main way in which government is called to account. They have powers to call witnesses and official papers so they can investigate government policy and actions thoroughly. They can achieve a great deal of publicity, especially the Public Accounts Committee. In recent years there have been influential reports on such matters as tax evasion and avoidance, and the weakness of controls over the banking system. e However, select committees have no powers to enforce any of their recommendations and there is no guarantee that Parliament as a whole will act on their reports. However, similar to the limitations of public bill committees, select committees still have a small research staff and may lack enough expertise to investigate effectively. It is also true that some members remain party loyalists so that sometimes their reports are not unanimous. This weakens their position, as does the fact that governments do not have to act on these reports and some committees work in relative anonymity.

That said, select committees have experienced something of a revival in strength and energy in recent decades. Reinvigorated under Margaret Thatcher in 1979, both the Norton Report (2000) and the Newton Report (2001) proposed a widening and a reinforcement of their remit and the Wright Committee (2010) called for further strengthening and legitimising — with the committee chair being elected by the Commons.

e Level 5 (21/25 marks awarded). a This answer is very good in terms of knowledge and understanding. b The student clearly understands the role of public bill and select committees and is able to analyse their role in the legislative process and evaluate their effectiveness, bringing out points in the extract while doing so. c There are some effective synoptic links, d along with some evidence of direct engagement with the extract and some precise exemplification. e Additional specific examples such as the work of the Public Accounts Committee in investigating the poor equipping of British troops in Afghanistan, the management of the BBC and the poor performance of parts of the NHS would have elevated the mark further.

■ 25-mark essay questions (AS and A-level)

These questions appear on both the AS Paper, where students must answer one such question, and A-level Paper 1, where you must answer two.

Which of the assessment objectives (AO) do they assess?

AO	AS	A-level
AO1	7	5
AO2	10	10
AO3	8	10

What do you need to do?

- Demonstrate a developed knowledge and understanding of relevant institutions, processes and concepts.
- Ensure that your response is clearly organised and analytical in style, arriving at a well-substantiated conclusion to the question posed.
- Offer a balanced and developed analysis of the issue at hand.
- Present and evaluate a range of perspectives on the issue at hand, using appropriately selected examples.

The prime minister and cabinet

'The UK prime minister has become too powerful.' Analyse and evaluate this statement.

ⓔ Higher-level responses will demonstrate a clear awareness of the fact that the prime minister is now seen to completely dominate the political system and that this dominance has been growing steadily since the 1960s. Analysis and evaluation will take account of a range of different prime ministers and balance these with the constraints, identifying synoptic links.

Student answer

The nature and scope of the UK prime minister has been the subject of intense debate for decades, if not centuries. The steady development of the role since the 1700s has resulted in a position for which no fixed set of responsibilities exists along with no clearly defined checks. Add to this the democratic hazards of an uncodified constitution, a majoritarian electoral system and an incomplete separation of powers and it is hardly surprising that questions arise as to whether the role has become too powerful. ⓐ

However, formidable checks do indeed exist. The capacity of the cabinet, the party, Parliament and the wider population to check prime ministerial power have all proved to be potent ones. It is perhaps the increasing tendency of prime ministers to adopt a presidential style and to be the sole spokesperson for government policy, separating themselves from the rest of government, that is seen as a key component in the argument that the role has become too powerful.

Prime ministers, especially since the 1960s, have made fuller use of their prerogative powers, especially their dominance of foreign and military policy and their use of patronage (note especially Tony Blair in Iraq in 2003). This has led many to conclude that there has been a structural shift in prime ministerial power — from a debate that centred on circumstances (particularly the size of a Commons majority and the charisma to utilise that position of strength effectively) to one that places the now substantial infrastructure at the disposal of the prime minister centre stage.

Prime ministers over recent decades have built up a large power base that includes the Cabinet Office, private advisers, policy units and the like. With the decline of mass political parties whose members had influence over policy, prime ministers tend to dominate the policy agenda to a greater extent than in the past. Cabinet has declined in importance and this has been matched by a growth in prime ministerial dominance of the cabinet.

However, any discussion of the prime minister would not be complete without a review of the extent to which executive power changed during the coalition years. **b** During 2010 to 2015, David Cameron's patronage powers were limited by the need to include Liberal Democrats in government, by the need to share the policy agenda with the Liberal Democrat leader and Deputy Prime Minister Nick Clegg, and by the fact that he did not enjoy a clear parliamentary majority. Cameron led a government which was always in danger of becoming divided and, under the delicate and unique circumstances of the coalition government, could rarely if ever rely on collective responsibility. **c**

Prime ministerial power is also constrained by the fact that the UK has less control over its own affairs than it used to. The EU is the main example of this, but the UK is also subject to international influence from such bodies as the European Court of Human Rights, the Council of Europe and NATO. Devolution has also reduced the jurisdiction of the prime minister.

All prime ministers' power is affected by factors beyond their control. These include various economic and military events and the fact that the attitudes of the media and the public may unaccountably change. In addition, prime ministers always run the risk of losing the support of Parliament and/or the cabinet. Thatcher, Blair, Major and Brown all suffered such losses of support. Prime ministers can be removed from office at any time by one of these bodies (unlike a fixed-term president).

Ultimately, for many commentators, while there has been a definitive shift in the executive power base towards the prime minister in a time of growing government complexity, this balance of powers and constraints is not constant but varies through time, events and the personality of the office holder.

e Level 5 (21/25 marks awarded). **a** This essay starts well, with many relevant conceptual points. **b** There are two distinct sides to the argument which stand up well to scrutiny **c** and the level of analysis is strong throughout. A drawback is the lack of synoptic links which the essay lends itself to — there were opportunities throughout to compare to presidential power, especially with regard to the personal bureaucracy that has developed over recent years.

The judiciary

'The role and the importance of the UK's most senior judges has grown considerably in recent years.' Analyse and evaluate this statement.

ⓔ Higher-level responses will not only identify some of the ways in which the role and importance of the senior judiciary in the UK could be said to have grown in recent years but also analyse and evaluate each of these areas with the use of examples and other evidence drawn from the student's own studies. There is likely to be a fully substantiated conclusion that follows on naturally from the discussion that precedes it.

Student answer

Most western democracies operate under a codified constitution, a body of fundamental law that is deeply entrenched, as well as being superior to regular statute enacted by the legislature. Under such systems judges — especially those sitting on a 'supreme court' — have the ability to review all actions, regulations and regular statutes against this fundamental law, and void or strike down as unconstitutional anything that is judged to be in violation of it. ⓐ Such is the case in the USA, for example, where the Supreme Court ruled that states could not impose an outright ban on abortion in the landmark *Roe* v *Wade* (1973) case, or criminalise someone for burning the American flag as part of a political protest, in *Texas* v *Johnson* (1989). ⓑ

In the absence of a codified constitution, the UK judiciary has traditionally been said to wield rather less power than its US counterpart. The doctrine of parliamentary sovereignty, and the ultimate supremacy of statute law over all other constitutional sources, means that the judiciary does not have the power to declare Acts of the Westminster Parliament unconstitutional — because they are, by their very nature, constitutional. ⓑ Thus the role of senior judges in the UK has traditionally been seen as determining whether or not government officials have operated within the authority given to them under an Act of Parliament, as opposed to questioning the constitutionality of the Act itself. These so-called ultra vires cases, though significant in many ways, rarely broke through into the mainstream media. Although some cases were of interest to those in the Westminster bubble, and to constitutional lawyers, the general public were largely unaware of their existence, let alone their significance. The most senior judges in the UK, those sitting on the Appellate Committee of the House of Lords, were hidden away from public view, with their work largely a mystery to all but those who knew them personally.

Three main developments are said to have led to a growth in the power of the UK's most senior judges in recent years: the advent of the Human Rights Act (1998); the explosion in EU laws and regulations; and the emergence and blossoming of the UK Supreme Court. ⓒ

By incorporating the ECHR into UK law, the Human Rights Act (HRA) allowed citizens to pursue cases under the ECHR through UK courts from October 2000. This move brought senior UK judges into open conflict with politicians in a number of areas of policy, most notably over the government's anti-terrorist measures, where the courts ruled that the indefinite detention of foreign terrorist suspects in the wake of 9/11 violated HRA guarantees of a fair trial and freedom from arbitrary arrest and imprisonment. The courts were equally dismissive of the government's Control Orders scheme and the attempts to curtail the protests of anti-war campaigner Brian Haw by imposing a wide cordon around the Palace of Westminster.

When the UK joined the European Economic Community (EEC) in January 1973, it also submitted itself to the authority of the founding document of that union, the Treaty of Rome, meaning that all UK law became subject to EEC law. For many years this simply meant that the UK government could be called to account at the European Court of Justice (ECJ). However, since the landmark Factortame case (1990), UK courts have been able to 'suspend' UK statutes that appear to violate EU law. This has become more significant as the scope and scale of EU operations has grown. Senior judges in the UK have effectively become the policemen of EU law, keeping a watchful eye over Westminster politicians.

Finally, we must consider the consequences of the creation of the UK Supreme Court under the Constitutional Reform Act (2005). Reducing the power of the Lord Chancellor, separating the UK's most senior judges from the legislature, and moving the UK's top court to its own building across Parliament Square had a symbolic significance that far outweighed any changes in form or function. Although the new Supreme Court essentially had no more powers than the 12 Law Lords it replaced when it first opened for business in October 2009, the enhanced public profile of Supreme Court justices and the media coverage of the Court's decisions have greatly enhanced its status and authority.

Therefore, while the most senior UK judges still operate within a system that by its very definition limits their power, and holds statute law and the power of Parliament above all else, their authority and influence can be seen to have grown significantly in the last 20–30 years. **d**

e **Level 5 (23/25 marks awarded).** **a** Starting with a paragraph which establishes context and sets out the ground rules for the discussion always helps to establish a clear pathway for the discussion ahead. This introduction performs that task very well indeed. **b** The student makes excellent synoptic links with other elements of the UK content and with material drawn from their study of the USA. **c** The clearly structured and analytical way in which the essay continues on from that point, through to the conclusion, is equally impressive. Each paragraph is clearly addressing a specific issue and the paragraphs are linked clearly and logically to form a whole. **d** There is a clear conclusion that follows on from the discussion that has gone before.

Knowledge check answers

1 Codified constitutions generally allow for greater clarity in the relationship between the state and its citizens, and between the institutions that make up the state. This means that it is easier to hold government to account, and for individuals to assert their rights.

Uncodified constitutions are far easier to change in times of emergency because they are un-entrenched. That means, for example, that major changes to the UK Constitution (such as the introduction of the Human Rights Act) can be made simply by passing an Act of Parliament.

2 It is wrong to describe the UK Constitution as unwritten because although it is not in the form of a single codified document, many of its sources are in fact written. Such written sources include statute law and a good deal of common law.

3 The UK was traditionally said to be a unitary state because sovereignty was held centrally and all subnational government was subject to the ultimate authority of the Westminster Parliament.

4 The UK is not a federal system because the Westminster Parliament is still regarded as sovereign and can therefore vary the powers granted to devolved institutions. Although legislation has been put in place to ensure that devolved institutions cannot be abolished without a referendum, that legislation could just as easily be repealed by the Westminster Parliament.

5 One reason it has been difficult to complete Lords reform is that the first phase reform resulted in a body that many see as highly effective as a revising chamber. Some fear that completing Lords reform might bring into question the superior status of the Commons. Others worry that the removal of many of those currently serving in the Lords would also see the loss of a wealth of parliamentary experience.

6 Prime ministers occasionally called general elections at a time when their party appeared well placed to win, even where a general election was perhaps not in the best interest of the country. The Fixed-term Parliaments Act was supposed to prevent that.

7 Although the courts can issue a declaration of incompatibility when the government has violated the HRA, they cannot strike down a law as 'unconstitutional'. This means that government and Parliament can, in theory, ignore the courts, as they did initially over the use of anti-terrorist control orders. In a similar way, although individuals can request information under the FOI, such requests do not always yield the information desired — and the appeals process is complex.

8 Entrenchment (literally 'dug in') means that a measure, in this case a Bill of Rights, is protected from being amended by a simple Act of Parliament. Entrenchment is difficult to achieve in the absence of a codified constitution that holds a higher status than regular statute law.

9 The Wright reforms recommended by the Wright Committee mean that select committee members are now elected by all MPs in the Commons and that chairs of select committees are similarly elected and paid an additional salary.

10 PMQs require the prime minister to be fully briefed on all aspects of government activity, good or bad. However, the televised session is seen as being light on in-depth debate and too heavy on media-friendly sound bites.

11 A government rarely loses a confidence vote because (a) the governing party usually holds a majority in the Commons and (b) such a motion would normally require all other MPs representing a diverse range of parties to vote in a single block.

12 Two main ways that the government is scrutinised are by public bill committees which scrutinise legislation and select committees which scrutinise the work of government departments.

13 This constitutional principle is an essential feature of the US Constitution, dictating that the various branches of government — legislature, executive and judiciary — should limit each other.

14 These parliamentary committees scrutinise the work of individual government departments and conduct their own research. The Home Affairs committee examines the work of the Home Office. In December 2016 it launched a major inquiry into UK immigration policy.

15 The House of Lords Act (1999) originally sought to remove all hereditary peers from the House of Lords (hereditary peers inherit their titles from their parents). The Cranbourne Compromise allowed 92 to remain in what was supposed to be a transitional chamber. In the absence of further reforms, these peers remain.

16 Passed in 2011, the Fixed-term Parliaments Act dictates that parliamentary elections must be held every five years, starting in 2015. With a two-thirds Commons majority, Theresa May proved that it remains within the power of the prime minister to call a general election.

17 This device is used by the government to cut short parliamentary or committee debate by forcing a vote on a proposal or legislative amendment.

18 Two ways that the Commons has changed its composition is in the significant increase in women MPs and the number of ethnic minority MPs.

19 Those MPs with ministerial or shadow ministerial positions sit on the frontbenches. 'Ordinary' MPs with no government responsibilities populate the backbenches.

20 Collective cabinet responsibility is the convention requiring members of the UK cabinet to stand publicly by all decisions made within cabinet.

21 Majority governments are the basis of the parliamentary process. However, even during the 2010–15 coalition, the legitimacy of the prime ministerial position of David Cameron as leader of the largest (minority) party was never contested.

22 In the UK the monarch is head of state, though largely in a ceremonial capacity — what Walter Bagehot referred to as a 'dignified' part of the UK's constitutional arrangements.

23 In charge of the Prime Minister's Office, the chief of staff coordinates the units within the Office and liaises between the prime minister and the rest of the cabinet.

24 Patronage powers relate to the numerous positions that are filled by the prime minister: cabinet ministers, bishops of the Church of England, peers, heads of various public bodies such as the BBC, as well as the nomination of individuals for honours.

25 Presidential prime minister is the term used to describe a much-debated expansion in the prime minister's role, involving a lack of proper consultation and a perceived disregard of Parliament.

26 The Cabinet Office (CO) is the civil service body that supports and coordinates the work of the cabinet, headed by the cabinet secretary. In recent years the CO has expanded, with many roles and personnel increasingly overlapping with the Prime Minister's Office.

27 Special advisers are political appointees made by a government minister to support their political agenda. A distinction is often made between special advisers and permanent, politically neutral civil servants.

28 The Ministerial Code is the document that sets out the rules and standards for ministerial behaviour in the UK.

29 Legal precedent is where a decision handed down by a senior court establishes a legal principle that is applied in all subsequent cases.

30 Judicial independence is the principle that judges should be able to perform their roles free from any public or political pressure or undue influence. Judicial neutrality is the principle that judges should apply the law fairly and consistently, without bias.

31 The current court consists largely of elderly men who were privately educated and have degrees from Oxford or Cambridge universities. However, it is only right that those serving in the highest court in the land should have studied at top universities. Moreover, Supreme Court justices will inevitably be of a certain age by virtue of the fact that they must first have served with distinction for a number of years in other judicial or legal positions.

32 The single case in question involves a US company, a piece of UK statute law, EU law and the concept of ultra vires. It illustrates the way in which the Supreme Court is routinely asked to arbitrate where different rules or regulations appear to be pulling in different directions.

33 The ECtHR is the body that enforces the European Convention on Human Rights. It is not an EU institution and operates under the Council of Europe. The ECJ is the court of the European Union. It hears cases arising out of EU law.

34 The case shows that in ultra vires rulings, the government always has the option of retrospectively changing the law in question to ensure that a minister is operating within their authority. Moreover, it shows that the courts have no power to force the government to change statute law in the wake of a declaration of compatibility. Essentially, Parliament retains sovereignty.

35 Repeatedly ignoring court rulings, although permitted, reflects badly on the government. It could appeal the case to the ECtHR and hope for a different outcome. It could also change the statute law in such a way as to remedy the error. Finally, it could withdraw entirely from the European Convention on Human Rights.

36 Although the HRA offers judges the opportunity to issue a declaration of incompatibility, they cannot strike down an Act of Parliament. This means that they are not on a par with their counterparts in the US Supreme Court.

However, by bringing the provisions of the ECHR into UK law, the HRA allowed individuals to pursue their grievances against the British government through the UK courts rather than having to go to the ECtHR in Strasbourg.

37 A unitary state is one where ultimate political power (i.e. sovereignty) is held by a single, central government. A federal state is one where sovereignty is shared by different tiers of government, each holding ultimate authority with their assigned spheres of operation.

38 The UK would effectively cease to exist as a single state if Scotland, Wales and Northern Ireland were, for example, able to negotiate separate treaties or go to war with foreign nations. Even in federal states such as the USA, individual states such as Texas are not permitted to enter into treaties or alliances with other countries. In contrast, policies on health and education can easily be delivered in a style and manner more suited to each of the nations that make up the union.

39 As well as now being a legal requirement before any such abolition can take place, a referendum might be seen as the 'right' thing to do for two distinct reasons. First, these institutions were initially created as a result of a 'Yes' vote in a referendum. Second, giving those people who would be most affected by such an abolition the opportunity to voice their democratic opinion gives the process greater legitimacy.

40 The phrase 'the Troubles' refers to the period of sectarian violence in Northern Ireland that ran from the 1960s through to the 1998 Good Friday Agreement.

41 Direct rule over Northern Ireland was re-imposed four times between 1998 and 2007. In most cases the imposition of direct rule came as a result of a failure to make sufficient progress against deadlines established as part of the peace process (e.g. over decommissioning of arms in 2000 and again in 2001).

42 Mebyon Kernow campaigns for devolution to Cornwall. The party argues that as Cornwall is an economically and culturally distinct region of the UK, the interests of Cornish people would be better served by a directly elected Cornish devolved assembly.

43 Combined authorities allow for cost savings because they enable officials to benefit from economies of scale when providing services. They also allow areas that have shared economic interests to coordinate their efforts in a manner that is in the interests of the region covered by the combined authority.

44 In addition to healthcare and education, there has been policy divergence in the structure and role of local government and, in the case of Scotland, in the electoral system used in electing local councils, with the introduction of the single transferable vote (STV). Recent years have also seen devolved institutions gaining more power over the setting of taxes, so there is likely to be further divergence in that area also in the near future.

A

accountability, ministers 10, 26, 43–44
Act of Settlement (1701) 7
Act of Union (1707) 59
Act of Union (1800) 63
A-level exam 71
    questions and answers 74–76, 81–89
anti-terrorism legislation 17, 19–20
AS exam 71
    questions and answers 72–73, 77–80, 86–89
assessment objectives 70
asymmetric devolution 11, 59
authoritative opinion 8

B

Backbench Business Committee 28, 32
backbenchers, role and influence 31–32, 38
Barnett formula 14–15, 69
bicameralism 26–27
Bill of Rights 20–21
Bill of Rights (1689) 7
bills 29
    committee scrutiny 23, 27, 83–85
Blair, Tony 39, 40, 45–46
Bogdanor, Vernon 68
Brexit
    and devolution 77–78
    referendum 15, 16
    and Supreme Court 58
Brown, Gordon 39
Burke, Edmund 30

C

Cabinet
    collective responsibility 44
    organisation and role 41–43, 74–75
    PM's relationship with 38, 42–43, 44–46, 79–80

cabinet committees 41
Cameron, David 38, 46
career politicians 33
Catholics, N. Ireland 64
checks and balances 26
civil law 48
civil liberties 15–16, 19–20
coalition government (Con/Lib Dem)
    constitutional reform 13–14, 33
    decision-making 46
codified constitutions 6, 72
collective responsibility 44
combined authorities 67–68
committees, parliamentary 22–24, 27, 32, 83–85
common law 8, 52–53
Commons Liaison Committee 23
Community Charge (Poll Tax) 45
confidence and supply deal 65
Conservative government, constitutional reform 14–15
Conservative–Lib Dem coalition
    constitutional reform 13–14, 33
    decision-making 46
Conservative Party
    confidence and supply deal with DUP 65
    Scottish 62
constitution (see also rights)
    change and reform (see also devolution) 10–15, 33, 51, 81–83
    codified 6
    principles 9–10, 49
    sources 7–8
    Supreme Court's position 52
    uncodified 6–8, 15–16, 72
constitutional monarchy 10
Constitutional Reform Act (2005) 11, 51, 52, 55–56
control orders 17, 20
conventions, constitutional 8, 36
core executive (see also Cabinet; prime minister)

components 35
    decision-making 41–46
    Parliament dominated by 33–34
    scrutiny 22–25, 39
Council of Europe 16
Court of Appeal 49
courts 48–49
criminal law 48
cronyism 31
crossbenchers 28

D

Davidson, Ruth 62
declarations of incompatibility 17, 20, 54, 75
delegates, representatives as 30
democracy 6
Democratic Unionist Party (DUP) 64, 65
derogation 17
devolution 11–12, 13–15, 46, 59
    England 65–68
    impact 68–69, 77–78
    Northern Ireland 11, 63–65
    Scotland 11, 13, 14, 59–62
    Wales 11, 13–14, 62–63
Dicey, A.V. 9, 16, 49
direct rule 64, 65

E

early day motions 24–25
ECHR 12–13, 16–17, 54, 55, 58
elected mayors 68
elections
    Scottish Parliament 59–60
    Welsh Assembly 62
    Westminster Parliament see general elections
elective dictatorship 33–34
English Parliament 66
English votes for English laws 14–15, 66
entrenchment 6, 19
e-petitions 25
European Communities Act (1972) 7

Index

European Convention on Human Rights (ECHR) 12–13, 16–17, 54, 55, 58
European Court of Human Rights (ECtHR) 16, 54, 58
European Court of Justice (ECJ) 16, 53, 58
European Union law 8
and Supreme Court 53–54, 56
European Union referendum 15, 40, 46
executive *see* core executive
expenses scandal 18, 29

F
Factortame case 18, 53
Falklands War 45
federalism 9, 12, 68, 77–78
First Lord of the Treasury 36
Fixed-term Parliaments Act (2011) 13
freedom *see* rights
Freedom of Information Act (2000) 18
fundamental law 6
fusion of powers 52

G
general elections
2017 46, 62, 65
intervals between 13
PMs influenced by 39
Good Friday Agreement (1998) 63–65
government
accountability *see* scrutiny of the executive
judiciary's relationship with 54–57, 75–76
limited 6
government departments 35
Greater London Authority 67
gridlock 26

H
hereditary peers 28, 31
House of Commons (*see also* MPs) 27

composition 30–31
PM from 36–37
political parties in 28
select committees 22–23
House of Lords
as appeal court 52
committees 23–24
composition 28, 31
Law Lords 51, 52
reform 12, 13, 33
role and influence 27, 32–33
Human Rights Act (1998) 12–13, 16–17
and Brexit 58
and Supreme Court power 54–55, 56
use and impact 19, 20–21

I
indefinite detention 17, 20
individual ministerial responsibility 43–44
inner cabinets 42
intergovernmental bodies, N. Ireland 64–65
IRA (Irish Republican Army) 64, 65
Ireland, home rule and partition 63

J
Judicial Appointments Commission 51
judicial review 8, 53, 75
judiciary
appointment 50–51
importance 55–56, 88–89
independence 20, 49–50
neutrality 49, 50
politicisation 57
role and powers 75–76
structure 48–49

L
Labour Party *see* New Labour
Law Lords 51, 52
laws *see* legislation
legal precedent 48, 52–53

legislation
anti-terrorism 17, 19–20
civil liberties threatened by 19
as constitutional source 7–8
EU 8
legislative powers, devolved institutions 60, 62–63, 64
legislative process 26–27, 29
backbench influence 31–32
committee role 23
peers' influence 32–33
liberties *see* civil liberties
life peers 28, 31
limited government 6
Locke, John 19
London, government 67

M
Magna Carta 7
Major, John 39, 45
mandate 30
May, Theresa 13, 39, 46
mayors, elected 68
McGuinness, Martin 65
ministers, individual and collective responsibility 43–44
monarchy
constitutional 10
declining power 36
MPs 27
as career politicians 33
expenses scandal 18, 29
parliamentary privilege 29
as representatives 30, 73
resemblance to electorate 30–31
role and influence 31–32, 38
MSPs 59–60

N
nationalists (N. Ireland) 63–64
negative rights 16
Neuberger, Lord 57
New Labour
constitutional reform 10–13, 33, 51, 59, 81–83

devolution programme 11–12, 59, 67

rights legislation 16–18

no-confidence motions 25

Northern Ireland, devolution 63–65

Northern Ireland Assembly 11, 64

Northern Ireland Executive 64

Northern Ireland peace process 45

O

Opposition, role 25

P

Paisley, Ian 65

Parliament (*see also* House of Commons; House of Lords)

bicameral structure 26–27

committees 22–24, 27, 32, 83–85

debates 24–25, 28–29

executive dominance 33–34

functions 22

legislative process 23, 26–27, 29, 31–32

powers reserved to 60, 77–78

representative function 30–31, 73

scrutiny of the executive 22–25, 38

Parliament Acts (1911/1949) 7, 33

parliamentary privilege 29

parliamentary sessions 24

parliamentary sovereignty 9, 26, 34, 68

patronage 33

peers (*see also* House of Lords) 28, 31, 32–33

policy divergence, and devolution 68–69

policy-making, PM's powers 44–46

political culture, and rights 18–19

political parties, in Parliament 28

Poll Tax 45

positive rights 16

power-sharing devolution 64

presidentialisation 40

primary legislative powers 60

prime minister

evolution of office 35–36

general election called by 13, 46

leadership style 39, 44–46

powers 33, 36–37, 37–40, 43, 86–87

presidentialisation 40

relationship with Cabinet 38, 42–43, 44–46, 79–80

role 37

Prime Minister's Office 37

Prime Minister's Questions (PMQs) 24, 32

primus inter pares 37, 38

private bills 29

Private Members' bills 29

privatisation 45

Protection of Freedoms Act (2012) 13

Protestants, N. Ireland 64, 65

Public Accounts Committee 22

public bill committees 23, 27, 83–85

public bills 29

Q

qualifying practitioners 51

quasi-federalism 12, 68, 77–78

quasi-legislative power 57

Question Time 24

R

referendums

Brexit 15, 40, 46

Scottish independence 40, 61

regional assemblies 67

Reilly v Secretary of State for Work and Pensions 55

representation 30–31, 73

resemblance theory 30

rights (*see also* Human Rights Act (1998)) 15–21

royal prerogative 8, 36

rule of law 9, 49

S

Salisbury Convention 33

Scotland, independence referendum 40, 61

Scotland Act (1998) 60

Scotland Act (2012) 13, 60, 61

Scotland Act (2016) 14, 61–62

Scottish government 60

Scottish National Party (SNP) 60, 61, 62

Scottish Parliament 11, 14, 59–62

scrutiny of the executive 22–25, 39

secondary legislative powers 62

second chambers (*see also* House of Lords) 26

select committees 22–23, 27, 32, 83–85

senior judiciary 50–51

separation of powers 36

Sinn Fein 65

SNP 60, 61, 62

sovereignty of parliament 9, 26, 34, 68

state 6

federal 9

unitary 9, 59

statute law 7–8

Stormont Parliament 64

Sturgeon, Nicola 60, 62

Supreme Court 48, 49

appointments to 51

Bexit impact 58

role and impact 52–58

T

terrorism prevention 17, 19–20

Thatcher, Margaret 44–45

Tigere v Secretary of State for Business, Innovation and Skills 55

trade unions 45

trustees, representatives as 30

U

ultra vires 53

uncodified constitutions 6–8, 15–16, 72

Index

unionists 63–64
unitary states 9, 59
United States of America v Nolan 54
unwritten constitutions 7
USA
    bicameralism 27

congressional committees 24
    presidential power 36, 40
    Supreme Court 52, 56

W

Wales Acts (2014/2017) 13–14, 63
Welsh Assembly 11, 62–63

Welsh government 63
West Lothian question 11, 66
Westminster *see* Parliament
Westminster model 10
West Wing 40
whips 27, 34